Collins

SNAP REVISION

CONFLICT
POETRY ANTHOLOGY

GCSE 9-1 English Literature

For Edexcel

PAUL BURNS

REVISE TRICKY
TOPICS IN A SNAP

SNAP REVISION

CONFLICT POETRY ANTHOLOGY

Published by Collins
An imprint of HarperCollins*Publishers*
1 London Bridge Street
London SE1 9GF

© HarperCollins*Publishers* Limited 2019

ISBN 9780008353063

First published 2019

10 9 8 7 6 5 4 3 2 1

British Library Cataloguing in Publication Data.

A CIP record of this book is available from the
British Library.

Commissioning Editors: Fiona McGlade and
Clare Souza
Project Editor: Katie Galloway
Author: Paul Burns
Typesetting: Jouve India Private Limited
Cover Designers: Kneath Associates and
Sarah Duxbury
Production: Karen Nulty
Printed in the UK by Martins the Printer Ltd.

ACKNOWLEDGEMENTS
p.28 *Half-Caste* copyright © John Agard 1996
reproduced by kind permission of John Agard
c/o Caroline Sheldon Literary Agency Ltd.
p.41 *Catrin* by Gillian Clarke, from *Selected
Poems* (Picador, 2016)
p.45 *War Photographer* by Carole Satyamurti,
from Stitching the Dar*k: New & Selected
Poems (Bloodaxe Books, 2005)*
p.49 'Belfast Confetti', By kind permission of
the author and The Gallery Press, Loughcrew,
Oldcastle, County Meath, Ireland from *From
There to Here* (2018)
p.53 *The Class Game* by Mary Casey
p.57 *Poppies* by Jane Weir (Templar Poetry)
p.62 *No Problem* by Benjamin Zephaniah,
from *To Do Wid Me: Benjamin Zephaniah Live
& Direct filmed by Pamela Robertson-Pearce
(Bloodaxe Books, 2012)*
p.66 'What Were They Like?' By Denise
Levertov, from POEMS 1960-1967, copyright
©1966 by Denise Levertov. Reprinted by
permission of New Directions Publishing Corp.
What Were They Like? by Denise Levertov,
from *New Selected Poems (Bloodaxe Books,
2003)*

The author and publisher are grateful to
the copyright holders for permission to use
quoted materials and images.

MIX
Paper from
responsible source

FSC
www.fsc.org **FSC™ C007454**

This book is produced from independently
certified FSC™ paper to ensure responsible
forest management.

For more information visit:
www.harpercollins.co.uk/green

Contents

A POISON TREE by William Blake

I was angry with my friend:
I told my wrath, my wrath did end.
I was angry with my foe:
I told it not, my wrath did grow.

5   And I water'd it in fears,
Night and morning with my tears;
And I sunned it with smiles,
And with soft deceitful wiles.

And it grew both day and night,
10   Till it bore an apple bright;
And my foe beheld it shine,
And he knew that it was mine,

And into my garden stole
When the night had veil'd the pole:
15   In the morning glad I see
My foe outstretch'd beneath the tree.

This poem is about...

a tree as a **symbol** of how anger and resentment can be cultivated and become fatal.

How does the first stanza introduce the theme of conflict?

The speaker, in simple language, recounts two different ways of dealing with anger. The first two lines describe how he has dealt with feelings of anger ('wrath') towards a friend. The simple act of telling his friend how he feels causes the anger to disappear. In contrast, the next two lines describe what happens when he is angry with someone whom he considers a 'foe' (enemy) rather than a friend. The two different ways of dealing with anger are summed up in the antithesis: 'I told my wrath, my wrath did end ... I told it not, my wrath did grow.' The failure to be open and honest causes the wrath to grow. This reflects Blake's belief in the dangerous effects of secrecy and the destructive nature of negative emotions. The final statement of the **stanza**, 'my wrath did grow', introduces the **extended metaphor** of the tree, representing the poet's anger. The fact that Blake gives no reason for his anger suggests that it is something trivial or that, whatever it might be, his reaction cannot be justified. It also gives a general application to the poem – any reader can easily identify with the feelings described.

The repetition of 'I' emphasises the essentially selfish nature of the poet's emotion, while the repetition of 'wrath' reinforces the strength of the emotion. The use of the word 'wrath', rather than 'anger', intensifies the feeling – it is one of the **seven deadly sins** of the Bible.

How does the second stanza develop the metaphor of the poison tree?

The first line of the second stanza introduces the idea that the poet is actively cultivating his anger. The use of the verb 'water'd' shows that he is willing the tree to grow. He does this by indulging in 'fears'. Again, he does not say what he is afraid of but his anger causes him deep emotion, the fears becoming 'tears', with which the tree can be watered. 'Night and morning' suggests that his anger has become an obsession, dominating his life. There is something secretive about the action of watering the tree, reflecting how he keeps his true emotions to himself.

Further developing the extended metaphor, he moves on from water to the other ingredient necessary for growth: sun. The third and fourth lines of the stanza describe his attitude towards his foe, who knows nothing of his anger. His 'smiles' are false, serving to increase his anger rather than lessen it. The soft sibilant sounds of 'sunned' and 'smiles', reflecting his outward demeanour towards his foe, continue with his 'soft deceitful wiles', indicating that he is setting out to trick his enemy.

By starting three out of four lines with the **conjunction** 'And' in this and the next stanza, Blake gives a sense of how his anger is building up relentlessly with barely a pause for breath.

How is the symbol of the tree developed in the third stanza?

The tree bears an apple, which is seen as attractive and something to be desired. It is 'bright' and 'my foe beheld it shine'. The use of the apple as a poisoned fruit recalls the Biblical story of Adam and Eve, where God tells the first humans that they can eat the fruit of any tree except for that of the tree of knowledge. Although the fruit is not described as an apple in the Bible, it is usually shown as such in art and the idea of a poisoned apple has become part of popular culture (for example in the fairy tale, *Snow White*). The poet's enemy is drawn to the apple just as Eve, encouraged by Satan, is drawn to the tree of knowledge. The poet might be identifying himself with Satan, the fallen angel, showing how much his 'wrath' has corrupted him.

The use of the phrase 'he knew that it was mine' at the end of the stanza suggests the foe is tempted not just by the value of the apple but also by the fact that it belongs to the speaker; he may be motivated by envy and by his own anger.

How are conflict and anger explored in the final stanza?

In the final stanza the poet again recalls the story of Adam and Eve by referring to his garden, referencing the Garden of Eden where Adam and Eve lived in innocence until they ate the fruit of the tree of knowledge and were banished by God.

The speaker's foe's actions are described as being secretive, the verb 'stole' suggesting the intention to steal the apple as well as describing the action of moving secretly. This action takes place under cover of darkness 'When the night had veil'd the pole', the **metaphor** 'veil'd **personifying** night as a force which enables a shameful, furtive action, hidden from view. This reinforces the idea of secrecy and shame as dangerous to the soul, recalling how the speaker's lack of openness about his anger caused it to grow in the first place.

The final two lines of the poem switch from past tense to present tense, adding to the sense of immediacy and the shock of the final statement. These lines show no remorse or reflection on the poet's actions. His emotions are expressed by the plain, one **syllable** adjective 'glad'. He is happy that his enemy is dead, 'outstretch'd beneath the tree'. This outcome is presented unemotionally and as a matter of fact. The tree, the symbol of his carefully cultivated anger, has caused his enemy's death. Just as the symbolic apple has poisoned the poet's enemy, the wrath which has not been 'told' has poisoned his own soul, leading to the ultimate act of destruction.

How does the poem's form contribute to how meaning is conveyed?

Like much of Blake's poetry, 'A Poison Tree' is deceptively simple in form, the **rhyming couplets** giving it an almost childlike feel. The four stanzas describe four stages in the development of his anger and its result. Most lines are written in trochaic tetrameters, the last foot of which is truncated so that the line ends on a stressed syllable. This adds to the strong, urgent **rhythm** of the **trochee**.

The exceptions are lines 2 and 4 of the first stanza and the final line, which have a much gentler, measured rhythm because of the use of iambic tetrameter. The change in the final line gives a sense that the poet's anger has gone.

Additional context to consider

Blake was an **early Romantic** poet. He used simple poetic forms and drew his **imagery** from nature. He is sometimes described as a **'mystic'** because he claimed to have visions and would make use of his spiritual experiences in his poetry and art. He disliked conventional religious and political institutions, believing both the Church and the state were **oppressive** forces.

Poetic links

- Use of the first person to express intense personal feelings in 'Cousin Kate', 'Half-caste', 'The Prelude', 'Catrin' or 'No Problem'.
- Use of imagery in 'Belfast Confetti', 'The Prelude', 'Poppies' or 'Half-caste'.
- Sense of triumph or defiance when facing enmity in 'The Destruction of Sennacherib', 'No Problem', 'The Class Game' or 'Cousin Kate'.
- Death of an enemy in 'The Man He Killed' or 'The Destruction of Sennacherib'.

Sample analysis

Both 'A Poison Tree' and 'The Man He Killed' tell stories about the killing of a 'foe' or enemy. Both use **ballad** forms, with regular **quatrains**, to tell apparently simple stories, which in fact look at complex moral issues. The speaker in Blake's poem does not tell us anything about the foe or why he considers him an enemy. Instead he focuses on the growth of his anger, using the extended metaphor of the tree. He 'water'd it in fears', associating the 'tears' of his emotion with the cultivation of his anger. The **sibilance** of 'sunned it with smiles' conveys the 'deceitful' way he acts towards his foe. Just as sun and water are essential for a tree to grow, fear and deceit encourage the growth of the 'poison' of conflict.

Although Hardy's form is similar to Blake's, the attitude shown to the 'foe' is different. The dash at the end of the first line of the third stanza, coming after 'because', indicates a pause for thought, a sense that he does not know why he shot the man. The second line gives the superficial answer 'Because he was my foe'. The following two lines, broken up by **caesuras**, suggest a questioning of the idea of the man being a 'foe'.

Questions

QUICK TEST
1. What is the difference between the speaker's response to feeling angry with a friend and an enemy?
2. What is the effect of the use of sibilance in the second stanza?
3. What happened to Adam and Eve when they ate the fruit of the tree of knowledge?
4. How could the poison tree be said to have poisoned the speaker as well as his enemy?

EXAM PRACTICE

Using one or two of the highlighted quotations to learn, write a paragraph exploring how Blake shows the effect of keeping anger hidden.

THE DESTRUCTION OF SENNACHERIB by Lord Byron

The Assyrian came down like the wolf on the fold,
And his cohorts were gleaming in purple and gold;
And the sheen of their spears was like stars on the sea,
When the blue wave rolls nightly on deep Galilee.

5   Like the leaves of the forest when Summer is green,
That host with their banners at sunset were seen:
Like the leaves of the forest when Autumn hath blown,
That host on the morrow lay wither'd and strown.

For the Angel of Death spread his wings on the blast,
10   And breathed in the face of the foe as he pass'd;
And the eyes of the sleepers wax'd deadly and chill,
And their hearts but once heaved, and for ever grew still!

And there lay the steed with his nostril all wide,
But through it there roll'd not the breath of his pride:
15   And the foam of his gasping lay white on the turf,
And cold as the spray of the rock-beating surf.

And there lay the rider distorted and pale,
With the dew on his brow and the rust on his mail;
And the tents were all silent, the banners alone,
20   The lances unlifted, the trumpet unblown.

And the widows of Ashur are loud in their wail,
And the idols are broke in the temple of Baal;
And the might of the Gentile, unsmote by the sword,
Hath melted like snow in the glance of the Lord!

This poem is about…

how God demonstrates his power and saves the city of Jerusalem by miraculously destroying the invading army of Sennacherib, the King of Assyria.

How does the first stanza establish the situation?

The poet refers to the king as 'The Assyrian', establishing his identity as the enemy of the Jewish people, and in a simile compares his actions to those of 'the wolf on the fold'. He is a wild and ruthless predator, while the people of Jerusalem are domesticated, innocent sheep, trapped in the 'fold' that is meant to protect them. His army is 'gleaming in purple and gold', the colours of royalty and wealth, emphasising its power and the impressive spectacle it makes. This vivid picture continues as the poet conveys the dazzling appearance of their spears in a simile comparing them to 'stars on the sea'. The Assyrians' power is again likened to the power of nature, as irresistible as the tide ('the blue wave').

What does the second stanza tell us about the Assyrians' attack?

The second stanza presents an antithesis. In the first two lines, the poet continues to use natural imagery to describe the army, this time comparing the soldiers to 'the leaves of the forest when Summer is green' as they march on the city at sunset. Using **anaphora**, the third and fourth lines again use the simile of the leaves but this time they are the leaves of autumn. Suddenly the fortunes of the Assyrians have been reversed and, apparently with no explanation, they lie 'wither'd and strown' on the ground.

How do the next three stanzas describe what has happened?

The poet reveals that the Assyrians have not been defeated by an army but by God's intervention, expressed as the 'Angel of Death'. This figure personifies both death and the power of God. According to Byron's Biblical source, during the night the Angel of the Lord entered the Assyrians' camp and killed the soldiers. Byron pictures the Angel of Death breathing on the Assyrians as he passes over them, instantly killing them. They are asleep when they die and Byron describes the eerie calm of the aftermath as their eyes 'wax'd deadly and chill'.

In the next two stanzas the poet goes into more detail about the scene of destruction. The fourth stanza describes a dead horse, focusing on the contrast between his power when alive, his 'nostril all wide' displaying 'the breath of his pride,' and his loss of power in death when the same wide nostrils show his weakness and suffering. In a vivid **simile**, the foam expelled by the dying animal is compared to sea spray, an image of the power of nature, but it is cold like death. The image of the horse illustrates the suddenness of the army's destruction and the loss of its power. The description of its dead rider in the fifth stanza develops this theme. The 'rust' on his armour contrasts with the 'gleaming' and 'sheen' of the first stanza, just as the 'still' soldiers with their 'chill' eyes and the 'white' and 'cold' of the horse contrast with the colour and movement of the invading army. The last two lines of the stanza describe a world with no human presence. Instead of the expected noise and violence of battle, the symbols of war ('banners… lances … trumpet') are still and silent.

How does the final stanza reflect the poem's themes?

The final stanza changes focus and describes the aftermath of the incident. The 'wail' of the 'widows of Ashur' introduces a human element to the poem, perhaps creating sympathy for the Assyrians who have been so ruthlessly destroyed. Their religion and culture have been shattered ('the idols are broke'). Their power ('the might of the Gentile') is described in a final simile, as having 'melted like snow', expressing how God is more powerful than both nature and great armies. There is a sense of both the futility of war and the temporary nature of human power, as thousands of lives have been wasted in Sennacherib's desire to conquer Jerusalem. The word 'glance' in the last line suggests that the Assyrian armies are only of passing interest to God and emphasises how much less powerful they are than Him. The final exclamation mark suggests wonder and excitement at His power.

How does the poem's form contribute to how meaning is conveyed?

The poem consists of six quatrains, each containing two rhyming couplets. Each line has four stressed syllables (tetrameter), the quick regular rhythm being created by the use of **anapaests** (two unstressed syllables followed by one stressed), which might reflect the beat of horses' hooves and the excitement of battle. The rhythm is occasionally slowed down by the replacement of an anapaest with an **iamb** (an unstressed syllable followed by a stressed syllable) at the beginning of a line (lines 6, 8, 10, 13, 14, 16, 17, 20 and 24).

The sense of excitement is also created by the constant repetition of 'And' at the beginning of lines, which drives the narrative forward.

Additional context to consider

Byron was a **Romantic** poet. The Romantics' interest in strong emotions and their expression through natural imagery are reflected here. This poem is based on an account in the Bible (2 Kings) of the invasion of **Judah** by the King of **Assyria**, Sennacherib. God promised Hezekiah, the King of Judah, that Jerusalem would be saved and the invading Assyrians were miraculously killed during the night before they could take Jerusalem. The freeing of the city from the Assyrian empire might **foreshadow** Byron's later commitment to Greece's fight for independence from the **Ottoman Empire**.

Poetic links

- Death in war in 'The Man He Killed', 'Exposure', 'What Were They Like?', 'Poppies' or 'The Charge of the Light Brigade'.
- Power of God or nature in 'The Prelude' or 'Exposure'.
- Conflict between cultures in 'Half-caste' or 'What Were They Like?'.

Sample analysis

'The Destruction of Sennacherib' and 'The Charge of the Light Brigade' present images of defeated armies. Byron rejoices in the defeat of the Assyrian army yet he begins the final stanza with an image of the effects of the defeat, focusing on 'the widows of Ashur' and their 'wail'. This implies sympathy for the victims of war, though his reference to the Assyrian gods as 'idols' makes it clear that, as in his Biblical source, the Assyrians are seen as the enemies of the true God, who has defeated them. The poet's use of the anapaest helps to convey a sense of excitement in the defeat of the enemy. The simile 'melted like snow' suggests the army's helplessness against the 'glance of the Lord'. The noun 'glance' implies an almost casual attitude on God's part, stressing both that He is all-seeing and **omnipotent**. The final exclamation mark confirms the poet's joy in the victory and conveys wonder at God's power.

Like Byron, Tennyson uses rhythm to convey the excitement of the battle, here dactylic dimeter. In his final stanza the stress on the first syllable of each line helps to create a tone of defiance and certainty, despite what has happened to the Brigade. The stanza begins with a **rhetorical question**, which might surprise the reader. 'Glory' would not normally be associated with a defeat but the poet challenges the reader with the idea that the Light Brigade's reputation should not 'fade'. He recalls the excitement of the 'wild charge', ending the second line with an exclamation mark, and then imposes on us the repeated **imperative** 'Honour'. His final line leaves us with no doubt about how we should view this defeated brigade. They are the 'Noble six hundred!' The final exclamation mark here, in contrast to the one that ends Byron's poem, proclaims the poet's admiration not of a victory, but of a glorious defeat.

Questions

QUICK TEST

1. To what is Sennacherib compared and why?
2. How does the simile of the leaves reflect the fate of the Assyrian army?
3. What symbols of war are shown to be unused in the fifth stanza?
4. What simile does Byron use to describe the Assyrians' loss of power?

EXAM PRACTICE

Using one or two of the highlighted quotations to learn, write a paragraph exploring how Byron uses the story of Sennacherib to demonstrate the power of God.

Extract from THE PRELUDE
by William Wordsworth

One summer evening (led by her) I found
A little boat tied to a willow tree
Within a rocky cove, its usual home.
Straight I unloosed her chain, and stepping in
5   Pushed from the shore. It was an act of stealth
And troubled pleasure, nor without the voice
Of mountain-echoes did my boat move on;
Leaving behind her still, on either side,
Small circles glittering idly in the moon,
10   Until they melted all into one track
Of sparkling light. But now, like one who rows,
Proud of his skill, to reach a chosen point
With an unswerving line, I fixed my view
Upon the summit of a craggy ridge,
15   The horizon's utmost boundary; far above
Was nothing but the stars and the grey sky.
She was an elfin pinnace; lustily
I dipped my oars into the silent lake,
And, as I rose upon the stroke, my boat
20   Went heaving through the water like a swan;
When, from behind that craggy steep till then
The horizon's bound, a huge peak, black and huge,
As if with voluntary power instinct,
Upreared its head. I struck and struck again,
25   And growing still in stature the grim shape
Towered up between me and the stars, and still,
For so it seemed, with purpose of its own
And measured motion like a living thing,
Strode after me. With trembling oars I turned,

30   And through the silent water stole my way

Back to the covert of the willow tree;

There in her mooring-place I left my bark, –

And through the meadows homeward went, in grave

And serious mood; but after I had seen

35   That spectacle, for many days, my brain

Worked with a dim and undetermined sense

Of unknown modes of being; o'er my thoughts

There hung a darkness, call it solitude

Or blank desertion. No familiar shapes

40   Remained, no pleasant images of trees,

Of sea or sky, no colours of green fields;

But huge and mighty forms, that do not live

Like living men, moved slowly through the mind

By day, and were a trouble to my dreams.

This poem is about…

an **epiphany** experienced by the poet when, as a child, he steals a boat and experiences the power of nature whilst rowing across a lake.

How does the poet begin his story (lines 1–11)?

Wordsworth begins his story by telling us when it happened ('One summer evening'), using the first person to relate his experience in the past tense and in **chronological order**. 'Led by her' personifies nature as a woman who is guiding the child. The scene he describes is peaceful and **idyllic**, the 'little boat' in the safety of the 'rocky cove'. His action is sudden and decisive, emphasised by the placing of the stark adverb 'Straight' at the beginning of line 4 and the urgency of the verb 'Pushed'. His action can be seen as liberating the boat ('I unloosed her chain') and perhaps himself. The caesura in line 5, indicated by a full stop, marks a break in the action and introduces the poet's reflection on his action. The lines 'an act of stealth/And troubled pleasure' suggest that he is feeling excited by the adventure but also guilty and as he sets out he hears 'the voice/Of mountain-echoes', **implying** that nature is aware of his crime.

His description focuses on the beauty of his surroundings, using the **literal imagery** of the light 'glittering idly' on the water to create a scene of magic and enchantment. The light forms a 'track/Of sparkling light' and seems to lead him on to his destination.

How does he describe his continuing journey (lines 11–20)?

The poet now focuses on the action of rowing, a change in mood and focus indicated by the caesura in line 11. He is 'Proud of his skill' and determined to reach his object, his strength of mind reflected in the adjectives 'proud', 'unswerving' and 'chosen', and the verb 'fixed'. He seems to be powerful and in control as he rows steadily, the rhythm of his action reflected in the regular iambic pentameter of the verse. He is in awe of the natural world that surrounds him, stressing the scale of what he sees: 'the summit' of the ridge; 'The horizon's utmost boundary'; 'far above'. Nature's vastness adds to its beauty and contrasts with his little boat, which he describes as 'elfin', the metaphor again suggesting a magical aspect to the experience. At this point, the poet seems at one with the beauty and power of nature, as he describes how he controls the boat, the steady iambic rhythm and **assonance** of 'as I rose upon the stroke' conveying control and calm. His strength in rowing the boat creates beauty, which he describes in a simile as 'heaving through the water like a swan'.

How does the mood change (lines 21–31)?

Suddenly a 'huge peak, black and huge' appears beyond the craggy ridge, which until now has been the furthest that the poet could see. Its colour contrasts with the image of the swan, and its size, emphasised by the repetition of 'huge,' is the antithesis of the 'elfin' boat. The peak is 'with voluntary power instinct'. It is personified and the image of its head 'Upreared' is threatening. This image shocks the poet and causes him to change from his gentle rowing to a more violent action, marked by the caesura in line 24. The repetition of the harsh-sounding **active verb** 'struck' underlines the violence of his actions, contrasting with the gentle 'dipped' and 'rose upon the stroke' earlier. The next few lines develop the image of the mountain as a threatening entity. It is not beautiful but 'grim' and it blocks out the beauty of the stars. Its size and threatening nature are conveyed by the metaphor 'towered'. It appears to him to move with a 'purpose of its own'. Unlike the gentle nature that led him to the boat, nature here is seen as powerful and violent.

How does the poet reflect on his experience (lines 29–43)?

Wordsworth describes how he fled from the vision of the mountain, returning the boat to its mooring place. The mood changes as he reflects on his experience, saying how much it disturbed him. He describes the 'darkness' of his thoughts and a feeling of 'solitude/Or blank desertion'. His whole view of the world, seen through his experience of nature, has changed. He uses anaphora to show what he has lost: 'No familiar shapes… no pleasant images of trees,/Of sea or sky, no colours of green fields'. A simple childlike delight in the natural world has been replaced by something darker, visualised in 'huge and mighty forms'.

How does the poem's form contribute to how meaning is conveyed?

The extract is taken from a long poem which traces Wordsworth's development as a poet. It represents a turning point in that process. It is written in blank verse, using regular iambic pentameter to reflect the poet's control over the boat and the action of rowing. The poet uses caesuras to mark changes of mood and action.

> ### Additional context to consider
>
> Wordsworth was a leading poet of the Romantic movement. This poem reflects the Romantics' concern with emotion over intellect and their interest in the power of nature. Part of an **autobiographical** poem, in which he analyses his emotions and the creative process, the extract describes an epiphany in his development as a poet.

Poetic links

- The power and beauty of nature in 'Exposure'; God's power expressed in nature in 'The Destruction of Sennacherib'.
- Powerlessness in 'War Photographer', 'Belfast Confetti', 'The Charge of the Light Brigade' or 'Half-caste'.
- Childhood and growing up from different viewpoints in 'Catrin', 'Poppies' or 'No Problem'.
- The experience of the writer or artist in 'Catrin', 'War Photographer' or 'Belfast Confetti'.

Sample analysis

Aspects of nature are personified as powerful forces in 'The Prelude' and 'Exposure'. The sudden appearance of the mountain and its effect on the poet in 'The Prelude' is conveyed by the **plosives** that start the single-syllable words 'bound', 'peak' and 'black', the latter two ending with the harsh sound of 'k'. The repetition of the adjective 'huge' emphasises the peak's size and almost suggests that the poet is so overwhelmed by it that he cannot think of any other word to describe it. He refers to its power as 'voluntary', personifying it as having a human-like will. The active verb 'Upreared' reinforces the sense that it is threatening.

Similarly, Owen personifies the wind. In keeping with his setting in the trenches, he imagines it as a 'merciless' enemy. The verb 'knive' conveys both the feeling of a cold wind and its potentially lethal effect on the men. Dawn is also personified as an enemy. Usually a symbol of hope, here dawn 'attacks' the soldiers with her 'army'. The metaphor gains strength from the fact that the men are awaiting an attack (which does not come) by an actual army. Unlike the perceived threat of Wordsworth's peak, the danger here is real and the men die because of the cold weather that causes the 'exposure' of the title.

Questions

QUICK TEST

1. How does the poet feel when he steals the boat?
2. To what two things does Wordsworth compare the little boat?
3. How does Wordsworth convey his feeling that the mountain is threatening?
4. How has his attitude to nature changed by the end of the poem?

EXAM PRACTICE

Using one or two of the highlighted quotations to learn, write a paragraph exploring how Wordsworth presents his feelings about the natural world.

THE MAN HE KILLED
by Thomas Hardy

'Had he and I but met
By some old ancient inn,
We should have sat us down to wet
Right many a nipperkin!

5   'But ranged as infantry,
And staring face to face,
I shot at him as he at me,
And killed him in his place.

'I shot him dead because –
10   Because he was my foe,
Just so: my foe of course he was;
That's clear enough; although

'He thought he'd 'list, perhaps,
Off-hand like – just as I –
15   Was out of work – had sold his traps –
No other reason why.

'Yes; quaint and curious war is!
You shoot a fellow down
You'd treat if met where any bar is,
20   Or help to half-a-crown.'

This poem is about...

a man telling the story of how he killed another man while serving as a soldier.

How does the poet establish the speaker's persona and his situation in the first stanza?

The use of speech marks, which enclose the whole poem, immediately establishes that Hardy is giving a voice to a character. This **persona** speaks in the first person and can be pictured speaking aloud. 'Had he and I but met' tells us that the persona is wondering 'what if?' – what if he and the other man had met under different circumstances? The reader will be aware, from the title, that he is talking about a man he killed so the everyday cosiness of the scene that the persona imagines seems **incongruous**. He imagines being friendly towards the other man and his use of **colloquial** language (for example the **tautological** 'old ancient' and the use of the phrase 'to wet/Right many a nipperkin' to describe having a few drinks) establishes him as an ordinary working man. The picture he presents is of two strangers meeting on equal terms and getting on well, with no reason for one to kill the other.

How do the second and third stanzas explain why the speaker killed the other man?

The first line of the second stanza presents us with the reality of how the two met, the conjunction 'But' setting up the contrast with the imagined scene of the first stanza. 'Ranged as infantry' places the two in a battle situation and 'staring face to face' shows us that they were on opposite sides and involved in close combat. The description of the action of killing is stark and expressed in plain language. There is no emotion, just a simple statement of the facts. 'I shot at him as he at me', a line consisting entirely of one-syllable words, shows the two men as equals, caught in a 'kill or be killed' situation. The speaker has killed the other man and survived but it could have been the other way round.

In the third stanza, the persona seeks to explain, to himself as well as to the reader, why he has killed the man. The dash at the end of line 9 indicates a pause for thought as he seeks an answer. The answer is simple: 'Because he was my foe'. Again, there is no emotion and no sense of any personal antipathy to the man. The next two lines are broken up by caesuras as the speaker considers what being a 'foe' means. The colloquial expressions 'Just so' and 'of course he was' suggest that it is simply a matter of fact. An ordinary soldier accepts that the men on the opposite side are the enemy. He does not question how or why they are. However, the last line of the third stanza suggests that the speaker is troubled by this. It starts with what might seem like a final statement: 'That's clear enough'. But this is not the end of the stanza. It is followed by another caesura, marked by a semi-colon, and the conjunction 'although', dangling at the end of the line. This suggests that the speaker is doubting and questioning what he has just stated.

How does the fourth stanza express the persona's feelings about the man he killed?

Hardy uses **enjambment** between the third and fourth stanzas to show the continuation of the speaker's thought process from 'although'. This stanza takes us back to the sentiments of the opening stanza and the idea that the man he killed was just an ordinary man, like himself. He imagines how the other man might have come to be at war, thinking that their circumstances were probably very similar and that the action of enlisting was 'off-hand', a casual decision with no thought for the consequences. The caesuras, marked by dashes, help to give the sense of real speech as he describes his own situation, which he thinks is similar to his enemy's. His motivation for enlisting is simple – his lack of work. The stanza ends with 'No other reason why', showing that for the ordinary man in the speaker's position, ideas about patriotism and justifications for war are irrelevant.

How does the final stanza reflect on war?

The speaker uses characteristic understatement to express the poet's feelings about the pointlessness of war. It is 'quaint and curious' – odd rather than tragic or even important. He uses the second-person pronoun 'you' to generalise his experience. This could have happened to anyone. He refers to the man he shot as 'a fellow', a colloquial term which suggests an equal, not an enemy, and returns to the image of the first stanza of drinking with him 'where any bar is', going further to suggest that he would show friendship by treating him and even giving him money.

How does the poem's form contribute to how meaning is conveyed?

The poem is arranged in five regular quatrains. Its form is similar to traditional ballad form, reflecting the origins of the speaker and the apparent simplicity of the story he tells. In each stanza all lines have three stressed syllables except for the third, which has four (usually in ballads the second and fourth lines have four stressed syllables). The **rhyme** scheme is also regular, line 1 rhyming with line 3 and line 2 with line 4 (*abab*). The poet uses caesuras effectively in the third and fourth stanzas, breaking up the regular rhythm and reflecting the speaker's thought process.

> ### Additional context to consider
>
> The poem was written in 1902, during the Second **Boer War**, but there are no specific references to that war, so the sentiments expressed could be those of any ordinary soldier in any war. Thomas Hardy's novels, stories and poems were usually set in his native Dorset and the persona here, who has been forced by poverty to sell his 'traps' and enlist in the army, can be seen as typical of the rural working men of the area.

Poetic links

- Victims of war in 'War Photographer', 'The Destruction of Sennacherib', 'What Were They Like?' or 'Exposure'.
- Soldiers in 'The Destruction of Sennacherib', 'The Charge of the Light Brigade', 'Exposure' or 'Poppies'.
- Voices of the powerless or oppressed in 'Cousin Kate', 'No Problem', 'Half-caste' or 'The Class Game'.

Sample analysis

In both 'The Man He Killed' and 'War Photographer' the speakers try to make sense of the experience of war. Hardy's persona is presented as an ordinary working man who has killed an enemy soldier. He imagines his 'foe' enlisted 'Off-hand'. This colloquial phrase suggests that the dead man and the speaker became soldiers almost by chance. His motivation for enlisting is simple. He was 'out of work', motivated by lack of money, so poor that he 'had sold his traps'. The reference to the 'traps' places the speaker as a countryman, possibly a **gamekeeper** or even a **poacher**. He identifies 'the man he killed' as being the same as him. There was 'No other reason' for either of them to go to war, by implication no good reason for war at all.

Satyamurti's **eponymous** war photographer seeks to make sense of war for those who see the photograph, to 'convince you/this is how things are'. The poem describes how he or she has captured an image of a 'little mother', the adjective suggesting vulnerability and the noun suggesting care that, in the words of the first stanza, 'lifts the heart.' However, this is not the whole truth as after the picture was taken the girl 'dropped her burden', the baby now dehumanised as something that can be discarded in the interests of self-preservation. The message is that 'hell' or war is 'untidy' and attempts to make sense of it are dishonest.

Questions

QUICK TEST

1. How does Hardy create the impression that the persona is chatting to the reader?
2. Which word in the second stanza tells us that the man was a soldier?
3. What reason does the speaker give for killing the other man?
4. What do we learn about the persona's background?

EXAM PRACTICE

Using one or two of the highlighted quotations to learn, write a paragraph exploring how Hardy presents ideas about war.

COUSIN KATE by Christina Rossetti

I was a cottage-maiden
    Hardened by sun and air,
Contented with my cottage-mates,
    Not mindful I was fair.
5 Why did a great lord find me out
    And praise my flaxen hair?
Why did a great lord find me out
    To fill my heart with care?

He lured me to his palace-home –
10   Woe's me for joy thereof –
To lead a shameless shameful life,
    His plaything and his love.
He wore me like a golden knot,
    He changed me like a glove:
15 So now I moan an unclean thing
    Who might have been a dove.

O Lady Kate, my Cousin Kate,
    You grow more fair than I:
He saw you at your father's gate,
20   Chose you and cast me by.
He watched your steps along the lane,
    Your sport among the rye:
He lifted you from mean estate
    To sit with him on high.

25 Because you were so good and pure
    He bound you with his ring:
    The neighbours call you good and pure,
    Call me an outcast thing.
    Even so I sit and howl in dust
30   You sit in gold and sing:
    Now which of us has tenderer heart?
    You had the stronger wing.

    O Cousin Kate, my love was true,
    Your love was writ in sand:
35 If he had fooled not me but you,
    If you stood where I stand,
    He had not won me with his love
    Nor bought me with his land:
    I would have spit into his face
40   And not have taken his hand.

    Yet I've a gift you have not got
    And seem not like to get:
    For all your clothes and wedding-ring
    I've little doubt you fret.
45 My fair-haired son, my shame, my pride,
    Cling closer, closer yet:
    Your sire would give broad lands for one
    To wear his coronet.

This poem is about...

the feelings of a woman who has been rejected by her lover in favour of her cousin, whom he has married.

How are the character and situation introduced?

Using the first person, the poet adopts the persona of a country girl ('a cottage-maiden'). The phrase 'Hardened by sun and air' gives the impression of a healthy, natural existence, while the phrase 'Not mindful I was fair' suggests that she was either unaware of her own beauty or just accepted it. The second quatrain of the first stanza consists of two rhetorical questions that introduce the idea of her seduction by asking why the 'great lord' noticed her. The strength of feeling invoked by this memory is conveyed by the repetition of the line 'Why did a great lord find me out', the first time followed by a seemingly **innocuous** memory of him praising her looks, the second presenting the result of his attention, which was to 'fill my heart with care'. Her life has suddenly changed for the worse.

How does the second stanza explore the persona's feelings about her new life?

The speaker describes a life of luxury, the result of her becoming the lord's mistress. The verb 'lured' implies that she has been tricked into living with him, almost as an animal might be trapped, although the noun phrase 'palace-home' suggests that his wealth was attractive to her. She interrupts her description of this life in the second line, expressing how she feels now ('Woe's me') but acknowledging that there was 'joy' in the life she led. The **ambiguity** of her attitude to her past is summed up in the **oxymoronic** 'shameless shameful life'. In retrospect, she takes the conventional view of her life as a mistress as 'shameful' but 'shameless' suggests that, at the time, she felt no guilt or shame. The nouns she uses to describe her relationship with the lord reinforce this ambiguity. The word 'plaything' implies that she meant nothing to him, **objectified** as a toy to be discarded. Yet she also calls herself 'his love', suggesting that he had genuine feelings for her. However, in the next two lines the poet uses two similes, which again objectify her. The simile 'like a golden knot' compares her to a valuable ornament. The phrase 'changed me like a glove' focuses on how easily he discarded her. In the last two lines of this stanza she expresses her feelings about this rejection. She still feels pain ('now I moan') and shame at what she did ('an unclean thing') and there is a wistful element of regret at what she might have been: 'a dove'. The dove represents purity, with **connotations** of peace and freedom.

How is Cousin Kate introduced in the third stanza?

There is a change in mood and focus as the persona addresses her cousin Kate. The first line tells us that Kate is now a 'lady'. She tells in simple terms how 'he' saw Kate, who is 'more fair' than the persona, and 'chose' and 'cast' away the speaker, the choice of verbs implying that the women are of no more value to him than objects. The second half of the stanza describes how he fell for Kate, presenting a rural idyll, a romantic view of poverty ('steps along the lane … sport among the rye'). Like a prince in a fairy tale, he raises her from 'mean estate/To sit with him on high'. At this point the persona could be telling the story of her own wooing by the lord but the next stanza reveals a crucial difference.

How do the next two stanzas explore the difference between the fate of the cousins?

The persona reveals that the lord has married Kate ('bound you with his ring'). The first line gives the reason for this. Unlike the persona, Kate is 'so good and pure'. The apparently complimentary and positive (in the context) adjectives carry a tone of bitterness. The phrase 'good and pure' is repeated in the third line, this time preceded by 'The neighbours call you', implying that the speaker herself does not agree. In contrast, they call her 'an outcast thing'. As in the second stanza, the speaker uses a **lexical field** of dirt and impurity to describe herself ('unclean', 'dust'). Then it was used in contrast with the 'dove' she might have been; now it is a contrast with the 'pure' Kate. However, Kate is described as sitting in gold and singing, like a captured bird.

The speaker's rhetorical question, 'which of us has tenderer heart?' implies that she thinks she is gentler and more loving than her apparently virtuous cousin. Her ambiguous attitude to her relationship is again apparent in her proud assertion that her 'love was true' while Kate's is temporary and weak, expressed in the metaphor 'writ in sand'. The speaker then considers what might have happened if the two women's roles had been reversed, if Kate had been 'fooled' into being the lord's mistress. She claims that she would not have married him, suggesting that Kate has married him for his wealth ('bought … with his land'). The stanza is characterised by a proud but bitter tone; the attitude to Kate is a mixture of jealousy and contempt.

How does the poem end?

The persona asserts her superiority to Kate and reveals a twist to the tale. She speaks of 'a gift you have not got', referring to Kate's material wealth and her status as a wife ('your clothes and wedding-ring') as she takes pleasure in feeling that Kate has reason to 'fret'. In the second half of the stanza she switches from addressing Kate to addressing her 'fair-haired son', revealing that she has had a child by the lord. **Paradoxically** he is both a source of 'shame' and 'pride' to her. The implication is that he is her 'shame' in the view of society while her own feelings are of 'pride,' not just in the boy himself but also in the fact that she has given birth to the lord's son, something Kate is unable to do. The final two lines are ambiguous. The idea that the child's father would give 'broad lands for one/ To wear his coronet' reinforces the idea that she has something of greater value than anything he or Kate can have. However, it could be that she is hinting that the boy is a bargaining tool and might one day 'wear his coronet'. These lines also show the ambiguity of her feelings about the lord. She loves his son as she loved him but seems happy that the lord cannot buy a child as he has apparently bought a wife. Her attitude is proud and defiant, her son representing her triumph over Cousin Kate.

How does the poem's form contribute to how meaning is conveyed?

The poem is a **dramatic monologue**, in which an invented persona tells her story. It is arranged in six stanzas of eight lines each. Each stanza contains two quatrains. This resembles the form of the **folk ballad**, usually a dramatic story told in a fairly simple way. The combination of ballad form with a first-person persona reflects the tone and content of the poem as the rejected mistress tells the story of her life.

Additional context to consider

Christina Rossetti was part of the **Pre-Raphaelite** movement and her poetry was inspired by historical (often medieval) subject matter. Although not set in a specific time or place, the story of Cousin Kate reads like a folk ballad. Its style also owes a lot to the poetry of the Romantics, like Wordsworth, who used the ballad form to give a voice to the experiences of ordinary people.

Poetic links

- Anger and bitterness in 'A Poison Tree', 'No Problem' or 'The Class Game'.
- Voices of victims/outsiders in 'No Problem', 'Half-caste' or 'The Class Game'.
- Female experience of relationships in 'Catrin' or 'Poppies'.
- Triumph over enemies in 'A Poison Tree' or 'The Destruction of Sennacherib'.

Sample analysis

The speakers in 'Cousin Kate' and 'Catrin' both directly address relatives with whom they are in conflict. Rossetti's persona uses the adjectives 'good and pure' to describe her cousin but they are spoken with bitter **irony**. Her apparent virtue meant the lord married her but that act is expressed as 'bound you with his ring', the word 'bound' suggesting that Kate is a prisoner. The difference between them is demonstrated by the contrast between the speaker's 'dust', worthless and dirty, and the 'gold' in which Kate sits. Yet there is a sense that Kate is worse off as the references to singing in gold have connotations of a bird singing in a cage.

Clarke also uses imagery to express her feelings about her relative: 'that old rope' (umbilical cord) binds her to her daughter – literally as she gives birth and metaphorically as the child grows up – just as the wedding ring symbolically binds Kate to her 'lord'. Clarke feels imprisoned by the 'tightening' rope. However, Clarke's symbol represents deep emotion and the unbreakable nature of the mother–child relationship. The rope was 'fought over' but 'neither won'. The **diction** of conflict conveys the strength and the ambiguity of her feelings about Catrin.

Questions

QUICK TEST

1. Which words in the second stanza show the lord does not value the speaker as a person?
2. How does the dove symbolise the life the speaker might have led?
3. Apart from the reader, who else does the speaker address?
4. What is the significance of the speaker referring to her son as a 'gift'?

EXAM PRACTICE

Using one or two of the highlighted quotations to learn, write a paragraph exploring how Rossetti presents the ambiguity of the persona's feelings towards the lord.

Excuse me
standing on one leg
I'm half-caste

Explain yuself
5   wha yu mean
when you say half-caste
yu mean when picasso
mix red an green
is a half-caste canvas/
10   explain yuself
wha yu mean
when yu say half-caste
yu mean when light an shadow
mix in de sky
15   is a half-caste weather/
well in dat case
england weather
nearly always half-caste
in fact some o dem cloud
20   half-caste till dem overcast
so spiteful dem dont want de sun pass
ah rass/
explain yuself
wha yu mean

25 when you say half-caste
yu mean tchaikovsky
sit down at dah piano
an mix a black key
wid a white key
30 is a half-caste symphony/

Explain yuself
wha yu mean
Ah listening to yu wid de keen
half of mih ear
35 Ah lookin at yu wid de keen
half of mih eye
and when I'm introduced to yu
I'm sure you'll understand
why I offer yu half-a-hand
40 an when I sleep at night
I close half-a-eye
consequently when I dream
I dream half-a-dream
an when moon begin to glow
45 I half-caste human being
cast half-a-shadow
but yu must come back tomorrow
wid de whole of yu eye
an de whole of yu ear
50 an de whole of yu mind

an I will tell yu
de other half
of my story

This poem is about...

the speaker (who can be identified with the poet) challenging the use of the **derogatory** term 'half-caste' to describe him, and asserting his identity.

How does the poet introduce the subject of his background and identity?

The term 'half-caste', which is also the poem's title, might shock some readers and be unfamiliar to others. Until recently it was commonly used to describe people of mixed race/ heritage but was often felt to be insulting. It has now largely fallen out of use but at the time the poem was written its use by a poet of that background would have had shock value.

The **tercet** that opens the poem establishes its tone, which is both humorous and challenging. The poet creates a bizarre picture of the speaker standing on one leg while having a polite conversation with his audience. This image draws attention to the oddity of the phrase 'half-caste', suggesting that it implies he is only half a person.

How does the poet develop his response to being called 'half-caste'?

The second, much longer, stanza opens with a direct address to the listener, using the imperative 'Explain yuself'. The phrase 'Explain yuself/wha yu mean' is repeated several times through the poem. Each time the poet suggests a new meaning or application for the phrase. The poet does not always use the spelling of **Standard English**, for example 'wha', 'dem' and 'dat', reflecting his own accent and asserting his identity. His first 'explanation' of the phrase turns it from an insult to something positive. Playing on the ideas of 'colour' and of mixed race being the mixture of people of different colours, he uses an image of a painting by Picasso, one of the great painters of the 20th century. He asks whether the mixing of red and green might result in a 'half-caste' canvas, in other words something less than the whole. The expected response, which he leaves to the audience, is clearly that the finished painting is beautiful because of the mix of colours.

His second image is based on nature, specifically weather. 'Light an shadow' has connotations of the differing skin tones of the 'half-caste' person's parents. The image suggests that the mixing of the two is a natural and positive thing, whereas the derogatory term 'half-caste' implies that it is unnatural. The next few lines talk about 'england weather/nearly always half-caste', implying that English people are in no position to criticise others. These lines could be read as **pathetic fallacy**, using the natural world to portray the feelings of people. The use of the word 'spiteful' briefly introduces a bitter tone to the poem, implicitly contrasting the English weather (and the English people) with the weather (and people) of the poet's native Guyana. This section ends with the **dialect** phrase 'ah rass', meaning 'my arse', an expletive which marks the speaker's increasing anger, albeit expressed in a humorous way.

The next section, again introduced by the **refrain** of 'explain yuself' returns to a calmer, more positive tone as the poet introduces an image of music. Again, he plays on the idea of 'half-caste' being a mixture of black and white by referring to piano keys, whose notes are mixed together to form music, such as that by Tchaikovsky. The idea of a 'half-caste symphony' is absurd as the word symphony means a harmonious coming together of sounds.

How does the poet change focus?

The next stanza opens with the repeated phrase 'Explain yuself/wha yu mean' but the focus moves from generalised ideas to the speaker himself. Throughout this stanza the word 'half' is repeated, emphasising the idea that calling someone 'half-caste' implies that he/she is less than a whole person and therefore inferior. The speaker focuses on his body, making a series of impossible statements: that he could listen with half an ear, look with half an eye (in both cases the 'keen' or sharp half), shake hands with half a hand or sleep with half an eye closed. He implies that the listener only values half of him but he clearly cannot use only that half as he is a whole person who cannot be divided. In this way, he ridicules attitudes to people like him. The poem ends with him telling the listener to return with 'de whole' of his/her eye, ear and mind. In this way, he turns the tables on those who call him a 'half-caste' by saying it is not he, but they, who do not see or hear clearly because they do not come with open minds.

How does the poem end?

In the final tercet the speaker promises to tell the listener 'de other half/of my story', asserting that there is much more to him than his identity as 'half-caste'.

How does the poem's form contribute to how meaning is conveyed?

The poem is written in free verse. It opens and closes with tercets, the first intriguing the audience and the second leaving them with something to think about. The two long stanzas each have a different focus, the first exploring the idea of being 'half-caste' through a series of images and the second expressing the absurdity of the idea by focusing on the speaker himself.

The lines are of irregular lengths and there are occasional rhymes but no regular rhyme scheme. This helps to give the poem a conversational tone, aided by the use of dialect, which reflects its origins as a poem to be performed. There is no punctuation except for the occasional solidus (slash), marking the end of a section, replacing the more conventional full stop or question mark. Together with the use of enjambment, this helps to give the impression of a spontaneous outpouring of thoughts and feelings.

Capital letters are used at the beginning of the first three stanzas but are not used to start sentences or for **proper nouns**. The poet does, however, use them for 'I' or its dialect equivalent 'Ah', possibly as a way of asserting his identity as an individual.

 Additional context to consider

The poem's theme reflects the poet's own background. Born in Guyana to a mixed-race couple, Agard emigrated to Britain in the 1970s. He is a **performance poet**, meaning he writes with the intention of reading his poetry aloud to audiences.

Poetic links

- Identity in 'Catrin', 'No Problem', 'Belfast Confetti' or 'The Class Game'.
- Use of imagery to describe experience and express feelings in 'The Prelude', 'Poppies', 'A Poison Tree', 'Belfast Confetti' or 'Exposure'.
- Direct address to/confrontation of the reader or listener in 'No Problem', 'The Man He Killed' or 'The Class Game'.
- The feeling of being an outsider in 'Cousin Kate', 'The Class Game' or 'No Problem'.

Sample analysis

'Half-caste' and 'A Poison Tree' use imagery to present strong feelings. Agard's title confronts the reader or audience with a term that they might find offensive and uses humour to challenge its meaning. He starts by presenting a ridiculous image of himself standing on one leg, the logical result of being half a person. Later, he returns to the idea of the half-person, the repetition of 'half' keeping the focus on his theme. He lists various parts of the body – the eye, the ear and the hand – to build a picture of someone incomplete. He links two of them to the term 'half-caste' by joining hyphens: 'half-a-hand' and 'half-a-eye'. In a play on words he suggests a 'half-caste' person might 'cast half-a-shadow'. His extended metaphor of the half person challenges the readers by making them laugh at the absurdity, as well as the ignorance, of their own prejudices.

Blake also uses an extended metaphor to express anger, though in 'A Poison Tree', far from confronting the person who has angered him, he describes what happens when emotions are repressed. The 'poison tree', which kills his 'foe', grows because it is cultivated by 'fears' instead of rain, and 'deceitful wiles' instead of the sun. As well as reflecting the process of cultivating a plant, Blake's metaphor has connotations of the tree of knowledge from which Adam and Eve ate, resulting in the banishment of mankind from Paradise.

Questions

QUICK TEST
1. Which phrase does Agard use as a refrain?
2. How do the images of Picasso's art and Tchaikovsky's music contradict the negative connotations of being 'half-caste'?
3. In what way are the lines about the weather (13–22) an example of pathetic fallacy?
4. What do the final lines imply about the attitude of the audience?

EXAM PRACTICE
Using one or two of the highlighted quotations to learn, write a paragraph exploring how Agard confronts the idea that he, as 'half-caste', is inferior to others.

Our brains ache, in the merciless iced east winds that knive us...
Wearied we keep awake because the night is silent...
Low, drooping flares confuse our memory of the salient...
Worried by silence, sentries whisper, curious, nervous,

5   But nothing happens.

Watching, we hear the mad gusts tugging on the wire,
Like twitching agonies of men among its brambles.
Northward, incessantly, the flickering gunnery rumbles,
Far off, like a dull rumour of some other war.

10   What are we doing here?

The poignant misery of dawn begins to grow...
We only know war lasts, rain soaks, and clouds sag stormy.
Dawn massing in the east her melancholy army
Attacks once more in ranks on shivering ranks of grey,

15   But nothing happens.

Sudden successive flights of bullets streak the silence.
Less deadly than the air that shudders black with snow,
With sidelong flowing flakes that flock, pause, and renew,
We watch them wandering up and down the wind's nonchalance,

20   But nothing happens.

Pale flakes with fingering stealth come feeling for our faces –
We cringe in holes, back on forgotten dreams, and stare,
snow-dazed,
Deep into grassier ditches. So we drowse, sun-dozed,
Littered with blossoms trickling where the blackbird fusses.
25   Is it that we are dying?

Slowly our ghosts drag home: glimpsing the sunk fires, glozed
With crusted dark-red jewels; crickets jingle there;
For hours the innocent mice rejoice: The house is theirs;
Shutters and doors, all closed: on us the doors are closed,–
30   We turn back to our dying.

Since we believe not otherwise can kind fires burn;
Nor ever suns smile true on child, or field, or fruit.
For God's invincible spring our love is made afraid;
Therefore, not loath, we lie out here; therefore were born,
35   For love of God seems dying.

Tonight, His frost will fasten on this mud and us,
Shrivelling many hands, puckering foreheads crisp.
The burying-party, picks and shovels in the shaking grasp,
Pause over half-known faces. All their eyes are ice,
40   But nothing happens.

This poem is about...

the experience of soldiers in the trenches of the First World War. They are dying, not because of enemy action but because of the conditions and weather, which result in exposure or hypothermia.

How does the poet introduce the soldiers' experience in the first two stanzas?

The poet places himself among the soldiers, sharing their pain by using the first-person plural in 'Our brains ache'. The use of the present tense adds to the immediacy of the experience. This phrase shows how the cold affects them mentally as well as physically. The weather is personified as a violent enemy – the winds attack 'mercilessly'. The sound of the wind is conveyed by the use of sibilance. The ellipsis at the end of each of the first three lines helps to convey the passage of time. Owen describes a time of inaction, of waiting, contrasting with the action they have experienced at the **salient** but still tense. In the fourth line **alliteration**, **onomatopoeia** and a series of commas vividly convey the nervous activity of the night-time trench. Four long lines are followed by a short line, 'But nothing happens'. This becomes a refrain, repeated at the end of stanzas three, four and eight.

The second stanza describes what the men can hear. Again the wind is personified, now 'mad' and violently 'tugging' on the protective wire. The noise it makes reminds them of the horror of men dying caught on barbed wire in 'twitching agonies'. In the darkness the sounds of nature are mingled with those of war as the men are reminded that the war never stops by the sound of the 'flickering gunnery'. The assonance of 'gunnery', 'rumbles' and 'dull' conveys a sense of heavy numbness in the reaction of the soldiers. They do not feel connected with the war and the poet asks a rhetorical question which could be about their current situation or the war itself: 'What are we doing here?'

How does the poet describe the dawn?

Usually symbolic of hope, here the dawn is described as 'poignant misery'. The idea that the soldiers' minds as well as bodies are numbed is demonstrated by the **triplet** explaining what they know: 'war lasts, rain soaks and clouds sag stormy'. Their thoughts and feelings do not reach beyond the present, the weather seeming to reflect the misery of the continuing war. Nature is again personified. Traditionally the dawn is personified as a woman but here she is the female commander of an army and, far from bringing hope, masses her 'melancholy army' – the sadness of her imaginary troops reflecting the mood of the real soldiers – and 'attacks'. Even this action, though, involves no excitement and the 'shivering ranks of grey', the soldiers in the trenches, do not react. The refrain underlines the continuing lack of action.

At the beginning of the fourth stanza, there is a flurry of action, the speed and sound of bullets conveyed by sibilance but even these do not change anything and are 'less deadly' than the weather. In a reversal of the norm, the sky is described as being 'black with snow' and the air, like the soldiers, 'shudders'. The relentless nature of the snow is emphasised by the poet's use of alliteration: 'flowing flakes that flock'. Both the snow, 'wandering up and down' and the wind, which is characterised by its 'nonchalance', reflect the boredom and indifference of the soldiers.

How does the poet write about death in the fifth and sixth stanzas?

The fifth stanza opens with more personification of the weather, this time depicting the snow as malign. 'Fingering stealth' has connotations of thieves and the alliteration of 'f' and 's' sounds give it a gentle yet disturbing tone, as if the soldiers are being tricked into sleep and, ultimately, death. They 'cringe in holes' like frightened animals but in the third and fourth lines the tone shifts as the poet describes an idyllic scene where nature is gentle and familiar, the 'blossoms trickling where the blackbird fusses'. These are images associated with spring and hope, but the stanza ends with a stark rhetorical question. The blossoms and blackbird may be the product of dreams or hallucination.

The sixth stanza develops this idea as the soldiers recall their homes in a vision where they are already dead and their ghosts visit their homes. The scene is one where humans no longer live and nature has taken over. It is a peaceful, even happy, scene as the crickets 'jingle' and 'innocent mice rejoice' in the house they have taken over but the fourth line tells us the soldiers will not return ('on us the doors are closed'). The short fifth line shows them accepting death. The refrain 'nothing happens' has now been replaced at the end of each stanza with a reference to the soldiers' deaths – the only thing that is happening.

How does the poem end?

In the seventh stanza the poet reflects on the reasons for the soldiers' death. Referring to the 'sunk fires' of the previous stanza, he says that 'kind' fires cannot burn unless they die. More than that, 'suns' will not be able to 'smile true'. This positive diction evokes an ideal world, reinforced by the triplet of nouns that follows – 'child, or field, or fruit'. These are all symbols of growth and life. He then introduces religion: 'God's invincible spring' associates God with nature – the benign nature of the spring, not the harsh nature that the soldiers are experiencing in the trenches. These lines suggest the war is necessary and the soldiers see their deaths as their fate and purpose: 'therefore were born'. The final line of the stanza is ambiguous. It might suggest that the soldiers are fighting for God and against a world that no longer loves Him. It might also suggest a sense of despair about the state of the world and perhaps even the death of God's love.

The first line of the final stanza identifies the frost as 'His', associating the harsh side of nature with God. God is responsible for the personified frost as Owen vividly describes its effect. He describes the actions of the 'burying party', 'shaking' from the cold. Their dead comrades are 'half-known', no longer individuals. The final line is broken by a caesura, giving greater impact to 'All their eyes are ice'. This can be taken literally, describing the ice that covers the eyes of the dead men, or as a metaphor for the burying party's lack of emotion. Owen then returns to the refrain, 'But nothing happens'. The war continues.

How does the poem's form contribute to how meaning is conveyed?

The poem is arranged in eight stanzas. Each consists of four long lines, followed by a much shorter one. The long lines are written, basically, in iambic hexameter, though the **metre** varies. Some lines start with a stressed syllable, for example line 6 and line 26. Many lines have an extra, unstressed syllable at the end. This softens the rhythm and adds to a sense of lethargy and the idea that the experience is continuing.

There is a regular *abba* rhyme scheme, though the poet often uses **half-rhyme** to soften line endings, giving the whole poem a gentler tone and adding a feeling of uncertainty.

Additional context to consider

Wilfred Owen served in the First World War, dying shortly before it ended in 1918. His poetry is based on personal experience and brought the reality of trench warfare to the public. Here he uses the first-person plural ('we', 'our', 'us') to identify with the soldiers and present their experience as a common one, shared by many.

Poetic links

- Soldiers in 'The Charge of the Light Brigade', 'The Destruction of Sennacherib', 'The Man He Killed' or 'Poppies'.
- Death and suffering in war in 'The Charge of the Light Brigade', 'The Man He Killed', 'War Photographer' or 'What Were They Like?'.
- The power of nature in 'The Prelude'.
- The power of God in 'The Destruction of Sennacherib'.

Sample analysis

'Exposure' and 'What Were They Like?' both use images of idyllic memories as a contrast to the devastation of war. In 'Exposure' this is as a vision or hallucination, ('forgotten dreams') of a typically English rural scene, at odds with the reality of the freezing trenches. The men 'drowse, sun-dozed' in their dreams, in stark contrast with reality where they 'stare, snow-dazed'. The **parallel phrasing** is enhanced by sibilance and alliteration of the harsher dental sounds. The men have dreams of the spring-time, with its connotations of new life and hope. The images are gentle and homely. The final short line of the fifth stanza asks whether it is for this dream of home that the men are dying.

This **nostalgic** tone is also present in 'What Were They Like?'. In the answer to question 5, the speaker reflects on rural life before war, suggesting it was hard. 'Rice and bamboo' sound basic, like their lives. However, the tone changes in the next two lines, which have a gentle, steady rhythm. The recurring 's' and 'f' sounds help to soften the tone. 'Peaceful clouds' is pathetic fallacy: the people and their way of life are peaceful. The expression 'stepped surely' gives a sense of security and confidence, which is shattered by bombs.

Questions

QUICK TEST

1. Which verbs are used in the first two stanzas to personify the wind?
2. What sentence does Owen use as a refrain?
3. What is unusual about the way Owen describes the dawn?
4. Which image in stanza six tells us that the men will never go home?

EXAM PRACTICE

Using one or two of the highlighted quotations to learn, write a paragraph exploring how Owen presents the suffering of men in the trenches.

THE CHARGE OF THE LIGHT BRIGADE by Alfred, Lord Tennyson

Half a league, half a league,
 Half a league onward,
All in the valley of Death
 Rode the six hundred.
5 'Forward, the Light Brigade!
Charge for the guns!' he said:
Into the valley of Death
 Rode the six hundred.

'Forward, the Light Brigade!'
10 Was there a man dismay'd?
Not tho' the soldier knew
 Some one had blunder'd.
Theirs not to make reply,
Theirs not to reason why,
15 Theirs but to do and die:
Into the valley of Death
 Rode the six hundred.

Cannon to right of them,
Cannon to left of them,
20 Cannon in front of them
 Volley'd and thunder'd;
Storm'd at with shot and shell,
Boldly they rode and well,
Into the jaws of Death,
25 Into the mouth of Hell
 Rode the six hundred.

Flash'd all their sabres bare,
Flash'd as they turn'd in air
Sabring the gunners there,
30 Charging an army, while
       All the world wonder'd:
Plunged in the battery smoke
Right thro' the line they broke;
Cossack and Russian
35 Reel'd from the sabre-stroke
       Shatter'd and sunder'd
Then they rode back, but not
Not the six hundred.

Cannon to right of them,
40 Cannon to left of them,
Cannon behind them
       Volley'd and thunder'd;
Storm'd at with shot and shell,
While horse and hero fell,
45 They that had fought so well
Came thro' the jaws of Death,
Back from the mouth of Hell,
All that was left of them,
       Left of six hundred.

50 When can their glory fade?
O the wild charge they made!
       All the world wonder'd.
Honour the charge they made!
Honour the Light Brigade,
       Noble six hundred!

This poem is about…

the bravery of the men of the Light Brigade who died heroically in a defeat by the Russian army during the **Crimean War**.

How does the opening stanza establish the situation?

The rhythm created by the poet's use of **dactyls**, combined with the repetition of the phrase 'half a league,' creates a sense of urgency and excitement, as well as reflecting the rhythm of the horses' hooves. The reader is plunged into the action. The phrase 'the valley of Death' strikes an ominous note, foretelling that this action will end in death. The fourth line introduces the refrain 'Rode the six hundred'. The repetition of this phrase throughout the poem keeps the actions and the fate of the men of the brigade at the forefront of the poem. The poet then introduces direct speech, quoting the words of the brigade's commander. The instruction that came down to 'charge for the guns' was a fatal error, giving the brigade no chance of success. Nevertheless, the command sounds positive and inspiring until Tennyson repeats the third line with an important variation. 'Into the valley of Death' shows the men riding towards their deaths, trapped in the valley.

How does the poet convey the action in the second and third stanzas?

At the beginning of the second stanza the poet repeats the words of the leader and asks the rhetorical question 'Was there a man dismay'd?'. The reader might be surprised by his answer. Even though the men are aware that 'Some one had blunder'd' and that they are probably riding towards their deaths, they still obey the order without question. The second part of the stanza explains why. Tennyson uses anaphora to convey their steadfast loyalty: 'theirs not'. This is reinforced by the rhyming triplet ending in 'reply', 'why' and 'die'. There is a sense of sadness at their powerlessness, mixed with admiration for their obedience and sacrifice.

In the third stanza anaphora is again used, here to emphasise the danger the soldiers are in, trapped by the 'cannon' that surround them. The sibilance of 'Storm'd at with shot and shell' reflects the sound of the missiles assaulting them. The use of the **passive verb** 'Storm'd at' shows their powerlessness in the face of overwhelming force. However, Tennyson shifts his focus to the men themselves with the repeated active verb 'rode', accompanied by two adjectives, 'boldly' and 'well', which emphasise their skill and bravery. This helps to make their action sound heroic and defiant. The poet uses personification to convey the horror of their situation. The valley is now identified with 'Death' and 'Hell', ready to devour the brigade.

How do the next two stanzas present the actions of the brigade?

In the fourth stanza the focus is on the actions of the British soldiers. The active verbs make their actions appear aggressive, brave and even glamorous: 'Flash'd', 'sabring', 'charging', 'plunged' and 'broke'. The charge is a magnificent spectacle and, in this stanza, there is a sense that it might succeed as 'Right thro' the line they broke'. A sense of suspense is conveyed in 'All the world wonder'd', an ambiguous phrase that could mean both that people wondered what would happen next and that they were in awe of the charge. It is the enemy ('Cossack and Russian') who are now under attack, the sibilance used to describe their fate, 'Shatter'd and sunder'd' recalling the 'shot and shell' with which they attacked the brigade. However, the brigade's success is short-lived as the **penultimate** line of the stanza soberly and simply describes their retreat ('Then they rode back') before the poet, for the first time, tellingly varies his refrain: 'Not the six hundred'.

After the excitement of the brigade's charge, the fifth stanza brings us back to the reality of the brigade's hopeless position by repeating the first five lines of the third stanza. Nothing has really changed and the assault from the cannons is relentless. The second half of the stanza also recalls the third stanza, but with some small yet significant variation. 'They that had fought so well' indicates that the action is over but the adverb 'well' survives from stanza three, suggesting that their action, though unsuccessful, is still praiseworthy. The references to Death and Hell remain with 'into' replaced by 'Came thro'' and 'Back from', suggesting amazement that they have survived, although the downbeat final two lines tell us in a simple way that they have suffered great losses. The word 'left' is picked up in the last line as the poet again varies his refrain, the mood now being one of sadness.

How does the poet reflect on the charge in the final stanza?

In the short final stanza, the poet reflects on what happened and how it should be remembered. He starts with a rhetorical question, asking when 'their glory' will 'fade', showing he has no doubt that the charge was glorious and that its memory will last a long time. The exclamatory 'O the wild charge they made!' recalls the excitement of the charge and he repeats the line 'All the world wonder'd', drawing attention to the fame of the action. He repeats the imperative 'Honour' to urge readers to remember the Light Brigade. To the poet, the blunder that started the action and its lack of success are irrelevant. The brigade itself must be remembered as glorious and 'noble'.

How does the poem's form contribute to how meaning is conveyed?

'The Charge of the Light Brigade' is a **narrative poem** in six stanzas. The six stanzas might be a reference to the six hundred men of the Light Brigade. The first five tell the story in chronological order. They vary in length, the longest being the fourth, which contains the climax of the story. The final stanza is the shortest.

The poem is driven by a strong, mostly regular rhythm. Most lines are in dactylic dimeter, which helps to convey the excitement of battle, the discipline of the troops, and the sound of the horses' hooves and artillery. The last line of each stanza is a refrain, identical in the first three stanzas but varied in the last three. These lines consist of a dactyl followed by a **spondee**, which halts the action, ending the stanza on a quieter, sombre note.

> ### Additional context to consider
>
> The charge took place during the Crimean War in 1854. The light cavalry was sent into action against Russian troops due to a misunderstanding of orders. They were overwhelmed and had to retreat after suffering heavy casualties. Tennyson, who was **poet laureate**, read about the battle in a newspaper. His poem reflects the public's admiration of the brigade's bravery and criticism of the commanders. This poem ends with a plea to 'Honour the Light Brigade' and has kept alive the memory of a battle that might otherwise have been forgotten.

Poetic links

- Soldiers in 'Exposure', 'The Destruction of Sennacherib', 'The Man He Killed' or 'Poppies'.
- Death and suffering in war in 'Exposure', 'The Man He Killed' or 'What Were They Like?'.
- Powerlessness in 'Belfast Confetti', 'Exposure' or 'No Problem'.
- Remembrance in 'Poppies' or 'War Photographer'.

Sample analysis

'The Charge of the Light Brigade' and 'Belfast Confetti' describe the experience of being trapped in a dangerous situation. In Tennyson's poem, the repetition of 'Into the valley of Death' as part of the refrain that closes most of the stanzas describes the actual physical setting for the charge and foreshadows the tragic end of the action by implying that it belongs to the personified 'Death'. In the third stanza the poet uses anaphora to show that the men are trapped, the repeated 'cannon' referring to the enemy's superior weaponry which is 'to right', 'to left' and 'in front', leaving the brigade with no escape except retreat. The active verbs 'volley'd and thunder'd' convey the violence of the assault. The emphasis, however, is on the men's bravery, shown in the adverbs 'boldly' and 'well'. There is no sense of them being afraid or panicking and they are more admired because they know that they are riding 'into the mouth of Hell'.

While Tennyson, using the third person, does not describe the men's feelings, Carson's first-person poem focuses on his reaction to the situation he finds himself in. His question 'Why can't I escape?' implies that, unlike the Light Brigade, he wants to escape. He finds himself in a 'labyrinth', which refers to the maze in classical mythology which housed the deadly **Minotaur**. This suggests that the maze of streets, which are familiar and should therefore be safe, could lead him to his death. In a strange but apt coincidence, these (real) streets are named after battles of the **Crimean War**. They recall the glory days of the British Empire. When he finds himself trapped in Crimea Street he is confronted by heavily armed troops, a situation not unlike that faced by the Light Brigade, surrounded by cannons in 'the valley of Death'.

Questions

QUICK TEST

1. How does Tennyson create a sense of the excitement of the battle in the first stanza?
2. What is the reaction of the soldiers to their realisation that a mistake has been made?
3. How does Tennyson convey the bravery of the brigade as it attacks the enemy?
4. Which verb in the final stanza tells us how Tennyson thinks we should remember the Light Brigade?

EXAM PRACTICE

Using one or two of the highlighted quotations to learn, write a paragraph exploring how Tennyson conveys the excitement and the tragedy of the charge.

I can remember you, child,
As I stood in a hot, white
Room at the window watching
The people and cars taking
5   Turn at the traffic lights.
I can remember you, our first
Fierce confrontation, the tight
Red rope of love which we both
Fought over. It was a square
10 Environmental blank, disinfected
Of paintings or toys. I wrote
All over the walls with my
Words, coloured the clean squares
With the wild, tender circles
15 Of our struggle to become
Separate. We want, we shouted,
To be two, to be ourselves.

Neither won nor lost the struggle
In the glass tank clouded with feelings
20 Which changed us both. Still I am fighting
You off, as you stand there
With your straight, strong, long
Brown hair and your rosy,
Defiant glare, bringing up
25 From the heart's pool that old rope,
Tightening about my life,
Trailing love and conflict,
As you ask may you skate
In the dark, for one more hour.

This poem is about...

a mother's relationship with her daughter and her memories of giving birth to her.

How does the poet set the scene for the memory of Catrin's birth (lines 1–5)?

The poem is written in the first person and from the first line the poet addresses the subject of her poem (Catrin) directly. Only the title uses the girl's name. In the first line she is addressed as 'child', emphasising the relationship above the girl's individual identity. A mother might also address a daughter as 'child' when telling her off. There is no affection expressed here.

The poet describes a room, which, it becomes clear, is the room in the hospital where she is waiting to give birth to the child. The 'hot, white/Room' is impersonal and uncomfortable. At this point it is not clear whether Catrin has been born but the poet remembers her as being in the room with her. However, her focus is on the view from the window – a dull, everyday view – so it seems that she is waiting to give birth.

How does the poet explore the struggle of childbirth (lines 6–17)?

Line 6 repeats 'I can remember you' and leads to a description of the baby's birth. She remembers it as a 'fierce confrontation', using a lexical field of conflict and war, as she does later with 'fought', 'struggle', and 'conflict'. At the centre of the poem is the ambiguous metaphor of 'the tight/Red rope of love'. This refers to the umbilical cord which connects the baby to the mother in the womb. The cord must be cut to separate the child from the mother: it is 'red' with blood. There is a paradox in the way the poet uses it as a metaphor: it is a symbol of love but they 'fought over' it. The pain and struggle of childbirth cannot be separated from the love that the mother feels for the child and it foreshadows their future relationship.

Line 10 is broken by a caesura, almost as if there is a pause in the woman's labour, as she switches her attention back to the room. She notes the lack of anything personal or emotional in the 'square/Environmental blank', particularly the lack of anything associated with children or creativity ('paintings or toys'), before returning to the pain and emotion of giving birth. The metaphor 'I wrote/All over the walls with my/Words' has connotations both of graffiti and the poet's profession as it describes how she shouts and screams during labour. She transforms the 'disinfected' space with the untidiness of raw emotion, summed up in the oxymoron of the 'wild, tender circles'. She uses the first-person plural ('our', 'we') to include the child, empathising with her 'struggle' as well as her own. She portrays the birth as a fight for independence and individuality by both of them: 'We want ... to be ourselves'.

How does the poet reflect on her relationship with her daughter (lines 18–29)?

The opening of the second stanza is calmer and suggests a **truce**: 'Neither won nor lost the struggle'. It might seem an odd, unemotional way for a mother to look back on the birth of her child and, as she switches to the present tense, she continues 'Still I am fighting/ You off' as if she resents her daughter. She does not give a reason for feeling conflict with the child, describing her in simple physical terms, except that she has a 'defiant glare'. The adjective is one often used to describe children and teenagers by frustrated parents. Combined with the noun 'glare' it suggests that Catrin is challenging her mother's authority. This experience brings back all the emotions the poet felt when she gave birth 'From the heart's pool'. The combination of two metaphors, the common 'heart' for love and 'pool' to express the depth of that emotion, conveys the strength of emotion she feels for her daughter. 'That old rope', the umbilical cord, might have been cut but it survives as a metaphor for their continuing close connection, which is still characterised by 'conflict' as well as by love, suggesting that the two are inextricably entwined.

The last two lines give the reader the reason for the current conflict between the poet and her daughter. She wants to 'skate/In the dark, for one more hour'. After the raw emotion and drama that the poet has been describing, this might seem like an **anti-climax**. It may be that skating in the dark is silly or even dangerous but, despite the 'defiant glare', she is not disobeying or violently challenging her mother. Indeed she asks politely, the **modal verb** 'may' showing her willingness to accept a refusal. The incident is certainly trivial, although the poet herself has said that she sees it as a romantic act of rebellion. Perhaps the poet has deliberately used a trivial incident to show just how overwhelming and intense, as well as contradictory, a mother's feelings towards her child can be and how a simple request, expressing a desire for independence, can affect a parent.

How does the poem's form contribute to how meaning is conveyed?

The poem is divided into two unequal stanzas. The first focuses on the birth of Catrin, as the poet addresses her daughter in the present but uses the past tense to describe the experience of childbirth. The second returns to the present day, using the present tense to describe a confrontation between mother and daughter. The poem is written in free verse, without rhyme or a strong rhythm, giving it a conversational feel. Within each verse paragraph Clarke uses enjambment when expressing strong emotions.

 Additional context to consider

Welsh poet Gillian Clarke's poems often focus on intensely personal experiences, using her own life to explore ideas about emotions and relationships. 'Catrin' is a **lyric poem**, addressed to its subject, exploring feelings that many readers might identify with.

Poetic links

- Identity in 'Half-caste', 'No Problem', 'Belfast Confetti' or 'The Class Game'.
- Use of imagery to describe emotion in 'The Prelude', 'Poppies', 'A Poison Tree', 'Belfast Confetti' or 'Exposure'.
- The experience of being a mother in 'Cousin Kate' or 'Poppies'.

Sample analysis

'Catrin' and 'Poppies' are both about the relationships between mothers and their children, and are both written from the mother's point of view. Clarke provides us with her daughter's name in the title but begins the poem by addressing her as 'child', an impersonal term that strips her of her individuality. Its use makes the neutral 'I can remember you' sound more like a woman admonishing her child than one sharing memories with her. Her description of the older Catrin is also lacking in individuality. Her 'straight, strong, long/Brown hair' could belong to a stranger. The adjectives 'strong' and 'straight' might also apply to her personality. This is picked up in the 'rosy,/Defiant glare'. The description could be that of any teenage girl. She is defined by her opposition to her mother. There may be a strong bond of love but the girl herself is not described or addressed with any affection.

Weir's memories are much more affectionate. The small, domestic actions she performs express her care for her son. She also uses the diction of conflict. The **juxtaposition** of 'Sellotape' and 'bandaged', while describing the way in which the Sellotape is wound around her hand, has connotations of the wounded, suggesting that the dangers of war are on her mind. However, here the conflict is not between them but in the outside world to which she releases him, like 'a song bird from its cage'. This image implies that she is resigned to his leaving, whatever might happen next.

Questions

QUICK TEST

1. Give three examples of words associated with conflict that Clarke uses in the poem.
2. What might the metaphor of writing on the walls be associated with?
3. What is the 'tight/Red rope' literally?
4. What does the metaphor of the rope convey about the mother's feelings for her daughter?

EXAM PRACTICE

Using one or two of the highlighted quotations to learn, write a paragraph exploring how Clarke presents conflict between parent and child.

WAR PHOTOGRAPHER
by Carole Satyamurti

The reassurance of the frame is flexible
– you can think that just outside it
people eat, sleep, love normally
while I seek out the tragic, the absurd,
5   to make a subject.
Or if the picture's such as lifts the heart
the firmness of the edges can convince you
this is how things are

– as when at Ascot once
10   I took a pair of peach, sun-gilded girls
rolling, silk-crumpled, on the grass
in champagne giggles

– as last week, when I followed a small girl
staggering down some devastated street,
15   hip thrust out under a baby's weight.
She saw me seeing her; my finger pressed.

At the corner, the first bomb of the morning
shattered the stones.
Instinct prevailing, she dropped her burden
20   and, mouth too small for her dark scream,
began to run...

The picture showed the little mother
the almost-smile. Their caption read
'Even in hell the human spirit
25   triumphs over all.'
but hell, like heaven, is untidy,
its boundaries
arbitrary as a blood stain on a wall.

This poem is about…

the work of a war photographer and how images can be misleading.

How does the poet introduce the work of a photographer?

The poet writes in the first person, adopting the persona of a professional photographer. We learn nothing about the photographer – not even whether it is a man or a woman – as s/he talks about photography in general terms. The photographer might be addressing a particular person or group of people ('you'). S/he starts with the image of a frame, saying that it gives 'reassurance' but that reassurance is 'flexible', before explaining two different ways in which that might work. People who see the photograph might use the fact that they can only see an isolated image or part of a bigger scene to reassure themselves that what they are seeing is unusual, while the rest of the world carries on 'normally'. They might take comfort from the idea that a photographer is interested in 'the tragic, the absurd', so the images need not be taken too seriously. On the other hand, some viewers might want to see an image as representing 'how things are'. Developing the image of the frame, the poet suggests that the 'firmness' of its borders reassures people that they are seeing something real, but only if the picture 'lifts the heart', making them feel happy or good.

What is the significance of the photographer's two anecdotes (lines 9–16)?

Satyamurti develops her theme by presenting two short **anecdotes** that give contrasting examples of the persona's work. The first tells of a photograph taken at Ascot, the race meeting, which is known for luxury and indulgence. In view of the title of the poem, this might come as a surprise. The photographer is a professional who takes pictures for money – not just a 'war photographer' with its connotations of danger and serious intent. The use of the metaphorical 'peach' to describe the girls suggests a **stereotypically** healthy English prettiness, while 'sun-gilded' has connotations of luxury and **privilege.** This is reinforced by the references to 'silk' and 'champagne'. 'Rolling' can suggest playfulness and/or drunkenness. The image could be seen as depicting the innocent fun of the young or the over-indulgence of the rich – or perhaps both.

The second anecdote presents a starkly different image, the antithesis of the first. Again the picture is of a 'girl' but she is 'staggering', not 'rolling' and she is pictured in 'some devastated street'. The scene could not be more different from Ascot, though we are not told where it is. The use of the **determiner** 'some' suggests that it could be anywhere – or perhaps that the experience, vaguely remembered, is not of great importance to the photographer. The girl carries a child and the photographer takes the picture. The caesura in the last line of the stanza represents the moment the picture is taken and the image frozen.

How do things change after the photograph has been taken (lines 17–21)?

The next stanza describes what happened after the image was captured, showing us what happens 'outside it'. The noun phrase 'the first bomb of the morning' conveys the scale of the violence that the girl and the photographer are caught up in. The short alliterative line 'shattered the stones' gives a sense of the suddenness of the incident. In her shock, the girl drops the baby, dehumanised as a 'burden'. Her frailty and powerlessness, previously hinted at when she was described as a 'small girl', are contrasted with the horror of the explosion, her mouth being 'too small for her dark scream'. The last line of this stanza consists of three words and an ellipsis, describing her action. She 'began to run...' It is a simple statement of fact. The ellipsis leaves us to wonder what might have happened next to the girl and to the baby.

How does the speaker reflect on the experience (lines 22–28)?

The final stanza focuses on the picture that the photographer took before the bomb went off. The phrase 'the little mother', the adjective implying vulnerability and the noun implying **nurture**, carries a tragic irony, as we know that just after this she dropped and, apparently, abandoned the baby. The use of the third-person possessive pronoun in the phrase 'Their caption' suggests that the photographer had no choice about the caption – it is based on how an editor has interpreted the image. This implies that the experience of war has been already interpreted for us by both the photographer and the editor. The caption focuses on a positive, something that 'lifts the heart', thereby offering 'reassurance' to the newspaper's readers.

The last three lines draw a message from the photographer's work. Life is not simple, bound by the frame of a photograph. Photographs do not always tell the whole story and can be interpreted in many ways. Life is 'untidy'. The final image contrasts the photograph with the reality of war – and life in general, 'its boundaries/arbitrary as a blood stain on a wall'. It is violent, shocking and much more complicated than anything that can be presented in a single image.

How does the poem's form contribute to how meaning is conveyed?

The poem is a dramatic monologue. It is divided into five stanzas of different lengths. It does not have a regular metre or rhyme scheme, although the poem ends by rhyming 'wall' with 'all'. The tone of the poem is conversational, the voice of the photographer giving his/her thoughts on photography, using examples of contrasting images.

Additional context to consider

Satyamurti is a sociologist as well as a poet. She writes about contemporary life and psychological and moral problems. The war referred to is not a specific one, though the image described may be familiar. The photograph of the girls at Ascot is also typical of those regularly published in newspapers.

Poetic links

- Victims of war/conflict in 'What Were They Like?', 'Poppies', 'Exposure', 'The Destruction of Sennacherib', 'Belfast Confetti' or 'The Man He Killed'.
- Social class in 'The Class Game'.
- Use of personae in 'Cousin Kate' or 'The Man He Killed'.
- Mothers in 'Catrin', 'Cousin Kate' or 'Poppies'.

Sample analysis

'War Photographer' and 'The Class Game' present images of privilege. Satyamurti's persona describes girls enjoying themselves at Ascot. This provides a contrast with the picture of the girl and the baby, which is the main subject of the poem, but it is used to make the same point about how people look at photographs for 'reassurance'. The setting brings to mind a scene of privilege and indulgence, and the images that follow confirm this idea. The girls are described as 'sun-gilded', a metaphor that has connotations of wealth. They wear silk and drink champagne, so are defined by luxuries. These are the **clichés** of privilege but the scene is open to interpretation. The girls may not live like this all the time and this could be a picture of innocent fun.

The clichés of privilege in 'The Class Game' are also there as a contrast, this time with the life of the speaker. The 'pretty little semi, out Wirral way' suggests a comfortable middle-class life rather than a life of luxury. It is contrasted with the speaker's 'corpy', the colloquial term for a council house, emphasising the speaker's class. She follows this with the colloquial expression 'not like some', addressed to the speaker. This suggests an attitude on the speaker's part that is a mixture of envy and contempt for the person she is addressing. There is no ambiguity about the clichés used here.

Questions

QUICK TEST

1. In which two ways does the frame of a photograph offer 'reassurance'?
2. What images convey the privilege of the girls at Ascot?
3. How does Satyamurti mark the moment the war photograph is taken?
4. Why is the photograph's caption inappropriate or inaccurate?

EXAM PRACTICE

Using one or two of the highlighted quotations to learn, write a paragraph exploring how Satyamurti uses photography to explore how people like to over-simplify life.

BELFAST CONFETTI
by Ciaran Carson

Suddenly as the riot squad moved in, it was raining
exclamation marks,
Nuts, bolts, nails, car-keys. A fount of broken type. And the
explosion.
Itself - an asterisk on the map. The hyphenated line, a burst
of rapid fire...
I was trying to complete a sentence in my head but it kept
stuttering,
5   All the alleyways and side streets blocked with stops and
colons.

I know this labyrinth so well - Balaclava, Raglan, Inkerman,
Odessa Street -
Why can't I escape? Every move is punctuated. Crimea
Street. Dead end again.
A Saracen. Kremlin-2 mesh. Makrolon face-shields. Walkie-
talkies. What is
My name? Where am I coming from? Where am I going? A
fusillade of question-marks.

This poem is about...

the poet finding himself caught up in a conflict between the army and rioters in his home city of Belfast.

How does the poet describe the experience of being caught up in the riot?

The term 'Belfast Confetti' is a **slang** term for the contents of homemade weapons and bombs, used during the 'Troubles' in Northern Ireland. There is irony and dark humour in describing things that are potentially lethal as confetti, the bits of paper traditionally thrown at weddings. The only thing the two have in common is that they are thrown.

The poem starts **in medias res**, the adverb 'suddenly' plunging the reader into the middle of a violent situation, which the poet goes on to describe in chronological order using the past tense. The 'riot squad', part of the British army, is attacked by the crowd. The poet uses the metaphor of 'exclamation marks', introducing the connection between writing and violence that will continue through the poem. As the punctuation mark that is used to express shock, surprise or strong feelings, the exclamation mark is an appropriate metaphor for the crowd's reaction. The second line tells us what the 'confetti' consists of with a list of four usually harmless – but now deadly – everyday objects: 'Nuts, bolts, nails and car-keys'. To describe them exploding, he returns to metaphor, again drawing on the lexical field of the mechanics of writing, 'A fount of broken type'. This line is broken up by two caesuras, marked by full stops, which give a sense of the panic induced by the action. The line ends with an incomplete sentence, 'And the explosion'.

The poet stops and visualises the bomb as it might be marked on a map – again using a punctuation mark as his metaphor, this time an asterisk, which resembles an explosion. As the army responds with bullets, he pictures them as a line of dashes, punctuation marks used to break up sentences, as the gunfire breaks up the riot. The fourth line explains to the reader what is going on in the poet's head, 'trying to complete a sentence'. The attempt at writing, putting thoughts in order, is disturbed by the noise of the violence around him so that the sentence (often defined as a phrase which is complete and makes sense) cannot be completed. He cannot make sense of what is going on. The present participle 'stuttering' could refer both to the sentence he is trying to form and the sound of the guns. The fifth line tells us that he is trapped, his way blocked. Again, he uses appropriate punctuation marks metaphorically: 'stops and colons'.

How does he describe his attempt to escape?

In the second stanza the poet switches to the present tense, giving a sense of immediacy and greater urgency. His description of the area of the city he is trapped in is paradoxical. A 'labyrinth' (originally the maze where the mythical monster the Minotaur was kept) is a maze from which it is difficult to escape yet he knows it 'so well'. It does not make sense to be trapped and lost in a place you know well. The names of the streets (real streets, including the one where the poet was brought up) recall the **Crimean War** of over a hundred years earlier, a war fought between the British and Russian Empires. The streets are part of everyday life but in the conflict their names add to the atmosphere of violence. It is ironic that those who live in streets named for British victories are now in conflict with the British state. The poet asks a rhetorical question, 'Why can't I escape?', which refers both to his situation at the moment and to the general situation. Why can he and others not escape their history and their background? The statement that 'Every move is punctuated' is reinforced by the poet's use of punctuation. There are four punctuation marks breaking up this line, stopping its flow just as the blocked streets stop the poet again and again.

The last two lines describe his encounter with the riot squad at the end of Crimea Street. The soldiers are described by the names of their equipment – sophisticated armoury and weaponry – in contrast to the rioters' 'Belfast confetti'. This dehumanises the soldiers and helps to make the experience impersonal, perhaps inhuman. The three questions in the last line are asked by the soldiers who stop him, though his use of first-person pronouns ('my', 'I') suggest that he is also asking them of himself, as he tries to make sense of what is going on. The final sentence unites the diction of writing and the diction of war in 'A fusillade of question-marks'.

How does the poem's form contribute to how meaning is conveyed?

The poem is written in free verse and is divided into two stanzas, more accurately described as verse paragraphs as they are not regular and are of different lengths. The first of these is written in the past tense. The second is in the present tense, suggesting the experience is not over, as we might have thought, but is happening now. The lines are unusually long but are frequently broken up by caesuras, reflecting the violent unpredictability of the experience.

Additional context to consider

Carson was born in Belfast and lived there throughout 'the Troubles', the lengthy period of conflict that started in the 1960s with tension between Catholic and Protestant communities. The British army was sent to keep the peace but violence escalated during the 1970s and continued into the early '90s, when this poem was written.

The imagery, taken from the mechanics of writing, reinforces the idea that this poem is about the poet's personal experience.

Poetic links

- Victims of war/conflict in 'What Were They Like?', 'Poppies', 'Exposure', 'The Destruction of Sennacherib', 'War Photographer', or 'The Man He Killed'.
- Identity in 'The Class Game', 'Half-caste', 'No Problem' or 'Catrin'.
- The perspective of the writer or artist in 'The Prelude', 'Catrin' or 'War Photographer'.
- The British army in 'The Charge of the Light Brigade', 'The Man He Killed', 'Exposure', 'Poppies' or 'No Problem'.
- Fear or a sense of powerlessness in 'The Prelude', 'Exposure' or 'No Problem'.

Sample analysis

'Belfast Confetti' and 'Exposure' use unusually long lines to convey the feelings of people caught in conflict. Carson's lines can contain as many as 21 syllables but there is no regular metre. The lack of regularity reflects the unpredictability of the situation. As the poet describes his experience the lines are broken up with caesuras, giving it a 'stop/start' feeling which reflects the experience of trying to escape. The second line contains three commas and three full stops. The full stop used to **end stop** the line appears to come too soon as the sentence 'And the explosion' is incomplete. Instead of using enjambment the poet makes us stop as he stops in response to the explosion. The next line is broken up with a dash, a full stop and a comma before ending with an ellipsis, which visually represents the bullets that have been fired.

Owen too uses ellipsis but in a more traditional way. His first three lines end this way, suggesting the passing of time during the night and the weariness of the men. The metre is basically iambic hexameter, but varied. The first syllable of a line is sometimes stressed, giving added importance to words like 'Sudden' and 'Watching'. The stress on 'Watch' suggests that the men are forcing themselves to pay attention. The stress on the first syllable of 'Sudden' has the same effect as Carson's use of 'Suddenly' as his first word. It demands attention both from the poet and the reader.

Questions

QUICK TEST

1. Why is the exclamation mark an appropriate metaphor for the crowd's reaction to the riot squad?

2. What other punctuation marks does the poet use as metaphors in the poem?

3. What is the significance of the use of the word 'labyrinth'?

4. What meaning do the final three questions have apart from their literal meaning?

EXAM PRACTICE

Using one or two of the highlighted quotations to learn, write a paragraph exploring how Carson expresses the fear and confusion of being caught up in a conflict.

THE CLASS GAME by Mary Casey

How can you tell what class I'm from?
I can talk posh like some
With an 'Olly in me mouth
Down me nose, wear an 'at not a scarf
5 With me second-hand clothes.
So why do you always wince when you hear
Me say 'Tara' to me 'Ma' instead of 'Bye Mummy dear'?
How can you tell what class I'm from?
'Cos we live in a corpy, not like some
10 In a pretty little semi, out Wirral way
And commute into Liverpool by train each day?
Or did I drop my unemployment card
Sitting on your patio (We have a yard)?
How can you tell what class I'm from?
15 Have I label on me head, and another on me bum?
Or is it because my hands are stained with toil?
Instead of soft lily-white with perfume and oil?
Don't I crook me little finger when I drink me tea
Say toilet instead of bog when I want to pee?
20 Why do you care what class I'm from?
Does it stick in your gullet like a sour plum?
Well, mate! A cleaner is me mother
A docker is me brother
Bread pudding is wet nelly
25 And me stomach is me belly
And I'm proud of the class that I come from.

This poem is about...

differences between people from different social classes, and the speaker's feelings about her background and how others respond to her.

How does the poet introduce the idea of class (lines 1–5)?

The title suggests that social class – the grouping of people according to their background, usually based on income and occupation – is unimportant and/or that people use it to compete with each other. The poem is in the first person and addresses a listener from a different background. It starts with a direct question asking the listener how he/she can 'tell what class [the speaker is] from'. The speaker then protests that she can, if she wants to, act like the listener, who is presumably middle-class. She gives two examples of how people decide on someone's class: speech and appearance. However, she does this in the accent or dialect of her class, using non-Standard English to ridicule the idea that she might want to appear 'posh' ('With an 'Olly in me mouth'). Her images of herself as a working-class woman and how she might pass as middle-class are simple and stereotypical, seeing the substitution of 'an 'at' for a headscarf as being enough to change perceptions.

How does the poet develop ideas about class (lines 6–19)?

The poet's next questions ask why the listener reacts as he/she does when the speaker uses the language of her class and region, saying "Tara' to me 'Ma". She contrasts this with the way she imagines a middle-class person speaks, the dated and stereotypical 'Bye Mummy dear'. She returns to her previous question of 'how', repeating the first line. This is followed by two antitheses, in the form of questions, contrasting her working-class life with middle-class life. Again, the examples are stereotypical. Her house, which she describes as a 'corpy' (Liverpool slang for a council house), is contrasted with a 'pretty little semi', which she places in the Wirral, associating that area with the privileged suburban middle-classes. This might be seen as a sweeping generalisation as crude as any she accuses her listener of making. She refers to her poverty by suggesting the listener might have deduced her background from seeing her 'unemployment card'. She contrasts the middle-class 'patio' with the working-class 'yard', the humour coming from the fact that they are basically the same thing, only the terminology being different.

She then repeats the first line and follows it with a series of questions, giving a list of things that might 'give away' her class. The first is deliberately absurd as well as challenging, asking whether she carries a label 'on me head and another on me bum'. The next four lines give examples of what might act as a 'label', indicating her class. Like elsewhere in the poem, the use of non-Standard grammar ('me' instead of 'my') and **vocabulary** ('bum', 'bog') suggests an attitude of defiance and pride in her background. She has said at the beginning that she can 'talk posh' but for the rest of the poem has refused to do so.

How does the focus change at the end of the poem (lines 20–26)?

At the start of this section the speaker varies her question from 'How' to 'Why', questioning the idea of social class itself. She follows this up with an aggressively worded second question, suggesting her being working class might 'stick in your gullet like a sour plum'. Here the harsh 'k' and 'g' sounds contribute to an aggressive tone. However, she does not expand on this idea or explain why she might think the middle-class listener should resent her or be offended by her background. She stops asking questions and, in the last five lines, expresses defiant pride in her background, starting with the exclamation 'Well, mate!', addressing the listener in a friendly, self-consciously working-class way.

In the final unpunctuated sentence she makes four statements, the first two about her family: dockers and cleaners are examples of unskilled people who work with their hands and are, therefore, working class. The fact that they are working (the docker in a job where numbers were being cut owing to changing work practices) and she is not reflects the economic situation of the time the poem was written. There was mass unemployment, particularly in areas like Merseyside where traditional industries were disappearing. There is also some irony in the fact that someone who writes of her pride in being 'working-class' is not working. The next two statements are examples of the differences between her language and the Standard English of her listener. The sentence ends with a declaration of her pride in her class and background, the tone positive and defiant.

How does the poem's form contribute to how meaning is conveyed?

The poem is not broken into stanzas but new thoughts are introduced by the four questions which end in 'what class I'm from'. This can be seen as a refrain. The lines are of irregular length, adding to the conversational (yet confrontational) tone. Except for lines 3 to 5, the poem is written in rhyming couplets. The simplicity of the rhyme scheme might reflect the simplicity of the sentiments expressed.

Additional context to consider

The poem first appeared in 1981 in a poetry magazine that featured the work of amateur, mostly working-class, poets – many of whom were beginners. The language and references reflect the writer's Liverpool background. The content of the poem draws heavily on stereotypical ideas about class that might seem outdated to many readers today.

Poetic links

- Outsiders in 'No Problem', 'Half-caste' or 'Cousin Kate'.
- Identity in 'Belfast Confetti', 'Half-caste', 'No Problem' or 'Catrin'.
- Strong opinions or emotions expressed in the first person in 'No Problem', 'Half-caste', 'Cousin Kate' or 'The Prelude'.
- Pride/defiance in 'The Charge of the Light Brigade', 'The Destruction of Sennacherib', 'Half-caste', 'Cousin Kate' or 'No Problem'.

Sample analysis

Both 'The Class Game' and 'Cousin Kate' end on a note of pride and defiance. Casey makes four simple statements about her social class, introduced by the familiar and consciously working-class 'Well, mate!' Her mother and brother's jobs mark them out as typically working class. The next two lines assert her use of dialect terms over Standard English, indicating her determination to be true to her background. The humour that comes from the sound of the local 'wet nelly' and 'belly' is enhanced by the use of a rhyming couplet. Casey uses her last line to declare that she is 'proud of the class that I come from'. This echoes the first line, where she asks how the listener can tell 'what class I'm from'. The change from question to statement implies that the speaker no longer cares about the listener's opinions.

The speaker in 'Cousin Kate' addresses her rival directly with the challenging 'I've a gift you have not got.' She asserts her superiority to her cousin, despite what others might think. By referring to her son as a 'gift' she compares him to the material gifts and the status which the 'lord' has given to Kate. In the middle of the stanza she reveals the identity of the gift by addressing her son directly. The oxymoronic 'my shame, my pride' conveys ambiguity but also defiance of society's expectation that she should be ashamed. The alliteration and repetition of 'Cling closer, closer yet' emphasises the intensity of her love.

Questions

QUICK TEST
1. What does the title imply about the concept of 'class'?
2. Give three examples of non-Standard English from the poem.
3. What do we learn about the person to whom the poem is addressed?
4. How would you describe the attitude of the speaker at the end of the poem?

EXAM PRACTICE
Using one or two of the highlighted quotations to learn, write a paragraph exploring how Casey presents her working-class background.

Three days before Armistice Sunday
and poppies had already been placed
on individual war graves. Before you left,
I pinned one onto your lapel, crimped petals,

5   spasms of paper red, disrupting a blockade
of yellow bias binding around your blazer.

Sellotape bandaged around my hand,
I rounded up as many white cat hairs
as I could, smoothed down your shirt's

10   upturned collar, steeled the softening
of my face. I wanted to graze my nose
across the tip of your nose, play at
being Eskimos like we did when
you were little. I resisted the impulse

15   to run my fingers through the gelled
blackthorns of your hair. All my words
flattened, rolled, turned into felt,
slowly melting. I was brave, as I walked
with you, to the front door, threw

20   it open, the world overflowing
like a treasure chest. A split second
and you were gone away, intoxicated.
After you'd gone I went into your bedroom,
released a song bird from its cage.
Later a single dove flew from the pear tree,
and this is where it has led me,
skirting the church yard walls, my stomach busy
making tucks, darts, pleats, hat-less, without
a winter coat or reinforcements of scarf, gloves.

30　On reaching the top of the hill I traced
　　the inscriptions on the war memorial,
　　leaned against it like a wishbone.
　　The dove pulled freely against the sky,
　　an ornamental stitch. I listened, hoping to hear
35　your playground voice catching on the wind.

This poem is about...

a mother saying goodbye to her son and thinking about those who have died in war. Whether her son has died, or is even involved in a war, is not clear (see page 60).

How does the poet introduce her themes?

The title suggests to the reader that the poem will be about war, loss and remembrance, because of the association of poppies with Remembrance Day, held on November 11th each year. The first line tells us that the poet is writing about an event that took place 'Three days before Armistice Sunday', a precise date, which reinforces the connotations of the title. The poppies have been placed 'on individual war graves', showing that people are remembering their loved ones, who have presumably died in action.

In the middle of the third line a caesura marks a change of focus. Now the poet addresses someone directly using the **second person**. The phrase 'before you left' does not tell us when or why the person left but its juxtaposition with the preceding sentence might suggest that the person has left to go to war.

As the speaker describes how she pinned a poppy to his (or possibly her) blazer, her action suggests a close relationship between them. She then introduces the lexical field of sewing ('crimped', 'bias', 'binding') from which many of her images will come. There are also nouns associated with war and violence. The 'blockade' of yellow has connotations of war, while the 'spasms' of red suggest the suffering of someone who has been shot or stabbed. These images might reinforce the idea that the person leaving is in the armed forces. On the other hand, the word 'blazer' is more often used for a school, rather than military, uniform. She could be remembering seeing him off to school – or she might be **conflating** two memories. It is not clear whether the events being described take place three days before Armistice Sunday or at an earlier time.

How does the poet express the speaker's feelings about the leave-taking (lines 7–22)?

The speaker continues to describe the leave-taking. As she does so we get a stronger sense of her being a mother, both from the way she fusses over the other person and from the earlier memories she relates about 'when you were little'. The object of her attention seems to be her son. She expresses her emotions through a mixture of images. The verb phrase 'rounded up' suggests a military operation, and 'steeled' has connotations of weaponry – swords or knives. In 'Sellotape bandaged' she brings together connotations of war (the injured being bandaged) with the everyday, functional 'Sellotape'. There is a rather odd **mixed metaphor** describing the inadequacy of her words: using another reference to textiles, she describes them as being 'turned into felt' yet also as 'slowly melting'. The references to sewing/textiles suggest how a mother might express love in a practical way, as she tries to control her emotions. The statement 'I was brave' carries some irony in the context. Although it is common to describe people as 'brave' when they are controlling their emotions, the speaker and the reader are aware of the bravery of those who have died in war. Then there is a sense of excitement at the possibilities life holds for her son, as she uses a simile to describe the world beyond her front door as 'overflowing like a treasure chest'.

How does the speaker react to her son's absence (lines 23–29)?

'After you'd gone' signals a change in mood. She releases a 'song bird from its cage' which could be a metaphor for her son finding his freedom and/or for her releasing her emotions. The bird imagery is picked up with 'a single dove', which could mean several things. The dove usually symbolises peace. Perhaps she feels peaceful; perhaps the war is over; or perhaps she is using the image ironically in the context that war is continuing. It might represent his soul, indicating that he has died. The **discourse marker** 'Later' indicates the passing of time, but how much? If the next event happens just after the son has left, then the whole episode has taken place just before or on the day she mentions at the start of the poem and she cannot have heard of his death. Or, it could indicate a longer passage of time, in which the beginning and end of the poem take place a long time after the leave-taking. How a reader interprets this affects the meaning of the rest of the poem.

The poet brings us back to the present day with 'this is where it has led me'. She returns to sewing metaphors to express her anxiety with a triplet of nouns ('tucks, darts, pleats'), before using literal imagery to describe her physical state, unprepared for the cold. Another military metaphor, 'reinforcements', is used to describe the protection she should, but does not, have from the weather and her feelings.

How does the poem end?

The poem ends with a six-line stanza, balancing the one at the start. It returns to the same place and time, but the speaker moves on to the 'war memorial'. Tracing the inscriptions suggests she is thinking about her son's name appearing on a memorial. She returns to the image of the dove and describes it in terms of sewing, the phrase 'an ornamental stitch' suggesting beauty but also uselessness, possibly implying that symbols of peace are just for show. The final line and a half do not resolve the poem's ambiguities. The poet ends with a poignant image of the speaker hoping to hear her son's 'playground voice catching on the wind'. She could be grieving for a dead son or she could be hoping that her living son is safe. The reference to the 'playground' might suggest she is remembering his childhood or it could mean that he is still at school and that the act of pinning a poppy to his blazer has made her think about how she might feel if she were to lose him.

How does the poem's form contribute to how meaning is conveyed?

The poem is written in free verse without a strong rhythm or rhyme scheme. It is written in the past tense as the speaker tells the story of saying goodbye to her son, but it is not clear whether she is recounting one event or several, or when the events described took place. The opening six-line stanza introduces the themes and situation, while the balancing six-line stanza at the end returns to the churchyard and the theme of remembrance.

Additional context to consider

Many readers of this poem assume it is about a woman mourning a son who has died in war. This may be because it was commissioned by the **poet laureate**, Carol Ann Duffy, as part of a collection of poems about the effects of war. However, there is little or no internal evidence to confirm that the speaker's son has died. It could just be that the act of pinning a poppy on his blazer has caused her to think about mothers who have lost their children in war.

Poetic links

- Remembrance in 'The Charge of the Light Brigade' or 'What Were They Like?'.
- Mothers and children in 'Cousin Kate', 'War Photographer' or 'Catrin'.
- Growing up in 'The Prelude', 'No Problem' or 'Catrin'.
- Victims of war in 'The Destruction of Sennacherib', 'The Man He Killed', 'Exposure', 'What Were They Like?', 'The Charge of the Light Brigade' or 'War Photographer'.

Sample analysis

'Poppies' and 'The Prelude' both use imagery to express feelings of fear or anxiety. 'Poppies' has a **motif** of sewing running throughout it. It is a skill that imposes order, and references to it help to control her emotions. After her son has left, her anxiety and fear for him take a physical form and she describes the feeling with three metaphors taken from sewing – 'tucks, darts, pleats' – effectively reflecting the physical symptoms of her fear. Unlike earlier, she is not in control of her son or her feelings. Her stomach is 'busy making' these alterations to her feelings, representing an instinct that she cannot control.

Similarly, in 'The Prelude' Wordsworth loses control. The feeling of power he gains from controlling his 'elfin pinnace' is suddenly destroyed by the appearance of the 'huge peak'. His panicked reaction is conveyed in the repetition of 'struck', the violence of the movement contrasting with the smooth control he had before. His fear is irrational but the personification of the mountain expresses how real it seemed. The fear of the speaker in 'Poppies' may also be irrational, depending on how the reader interprets her situation, but it is expressed in everyday metaphors which readers might easily identify with, whereas the images of powerful nature used by Wordsworth suggest that his fear is **existential** and special to him as a poet.

Questions

QUICK TEST

1. How does the setting described at the start of the poem reflect the poem's themes?
2. From which two lexical fields are most of the poem's images taken?
3. What is the significance of the release of the song bird?
4. What might the speaker be thinking about at the end of the poem?

EXAM PRACTICE

Using one or two of the highlighted quotations to learn, write a paragraph exploring how Weir presents the speaker's reaction to the loss of her son.

NO PROBLEM
by Benjamin Zephaniah

I am not de problem
But I bear de brunt
Of silly playground taunts
An racist stunts,
5 I am not de problem
I am born academic
But dey got me on de run
Now I am branded athletic
I am not de problem
10 If yu give I a chance
I can teach yu of Timbuktu
I can do more dan dance,
I am not de problem
I greet yu wid a smile
15 Yu put me in a pigeon hole
But I am versatile

These conditions may affect me
As I get older,
An I am positively sure
20 I have no chips on me shoulders,
Black is not de problem
Mother country get it right
An juss fe de record,
Sum of me best friends are white.

This poem is about…

a black person confronting the racist attitudes he encounters in British society.

How does the poet state his case in the first four lines?

The speaker identifies himself as someone who is considered a 'problem' by others but is, in fact, the victim of racism. Given the context of Zephaniah's own life and the fact that his poems are written to be read by him to an audience, it is clear that the speaker is either the poet himself or someone like him. The rest of the poem shows that he is representative of all black people in a predominantly white society. The speaker's identity as a person of Caribbean origin is reinforced by the use of dialect rather than Standard English, conveying the way he speaks: 'de' instead of 'the' and 'an' instead of 'and'.

The initial, defiant statement that the speaker is 'not de problem' sounds like an answer to people who have told him, or implied, that he is a problem to be dealt with. This statement is repeated at the beginning of every set of four lines. This time it is followed by a triplet of half-rhymes, which describes his experience, suggesting the problem is with those who bully him. In the noun phrase 'playground taunts', the use of the adjective 'playground' implies both the childishness of such behaviour and the fact that it begins at an early age. This is linked with the more serious 'racist stunts', showing that there is a link between what might seem 'silly' and what is clearly 'racist'. The adjective 'racist' makes clear the reason for his treatment, stating strongly his perception of the society he lives in.

What is his response to being considered a problem (lines 5–16)?

The next twelve lines contain three rhyming quatrains. Each one starts with the repeated line 'I am not de problem' and answers it with a positive statement about the speaker's character or abilities, which is then followed by a line describing how he (in common with all people of his **ethnicity**) is regarded by society.

He tells us that he is 'academic' in the first quatrain and in the second gives an example to illustrate his academic ability. The reference to 'Timbuktu' suggests not just his knowledge but the achievements of black people, as the city was once the centre of a wealthy African civilisation. It is also a place often used in the past by British people as an example of somewhere faraway and exotic, strange to the point where many people thought it was made up.

He suggests that (white) society ignores this part of his culture by using two examples of how other people stereotypically view the abilities of black people. Black people are assumed to be 'athletic'. In itself this is not insulting, but it is a stereotype and can be considered **patronising**. Zephaniah makes the serious point that black children can be encouraged to excel in sport at the expense of academic achievement. The idea that this is racist is emphasised by two phrases that have connotations of slavery. 'On de run' refers not just to sprinting but also to escaping slavery. The passive verb 'branded' reinforces this by referring to the practice of 'branding' slaves to show who they belonged to. The next quatrain contrasts the culture of Timbuktu with the widely held stereotype – again, often repeated by people who intend to be flattering rather than racist – that all black people can dance. The speaker insists that he 'can do more'. The next quatrain suggests that even showing a positive and friendly attitude 'wid a smile' can lead to him being put 'in a pigeon hole'. Patronising attitudes, even if well-meaning, judge him and limit him.

How does the speaker reflect on his experience (lines 17–24)?

The break between the two sections signals a change of focus as the speaker reflects on what these racist assumptions mean. The longer first line, written in Standard English, changes the tone to something more thoughtful, as he considers how 'These conditions' might influence him through life, though he does not expand on what effect – presumably a negative one – they will have. He then anticipates a reaction that he feels some of his listeners/readers might have to what he has said. The common metaphorical saying about having a chip on one's shoulder refers to holding a grudge and using perceived bad treatment as a reason for aggressive argument. He is 'positively sure' that this is not the case. In the final quatrain he challenges British society to 'get it right', He refers ironically to Britain as the 'Mother country', a phrase used in **colonial** times to suggest that Britain was benign and welcoming to people from the Empire. He then defuses the sense of anger and challenge a little in the final line. This inverts a saying ('some of my best friends are black') commonly considered to be used by white people who want to deny that they are racist. He leaves his audience with a joke, but one that is designed to make them think.

How does the poem's form contribute to how meaning is conveyed?

The poem is divided into two verse stanzas of unequal length. The lines are of unequal length, though mostly short. Most lines contain three or four stressed syllables, sometimes iambic and sometimes trochaic. This gives the poem a lively, but irregular, rhythm.

There is little punctuation, with the occasional line end-stopped with a comma at a point when a full stop would normally be used, marking where the speaker might pause for breath. Zephaniah makes a lot of use of rhyme. The rhyme scheme is regular (*abcb*), creating quatrains. All this gives the poem a lively, often humorous, tone with a sense of unpredictability, reflecting its origins as a poem to be performed.

Additional context to consider

Zephaniah's background influences both the content and the tone of this poem. He was born in Birmingham and brought up partly there and partly in Jamaica. He had a difficult childhood and no academic success but later had great success as a performance poet. The speaker in the poem is a representative of all black people in Britain but both the anger and the humour are the poet's own.

Poetic links

- Identity and individuality in 'Half-caste', 'Catrin' or 'The Class Game'.
- The British Empire and its aftermath in 'The Charge of the Light Brigade', 'The Man He Killed', 'Half-caste', 'Belfast Confetti' or 'Poppies'.
- Growing up in 'The Prelude', 'Poppies' or 'Catrin'.
- A sense of being an outsider in 'Cousin Kate', 'The Class Game' or 'Half-caste'.
- Pride and defiance in 'The Charge of the Light Brigade', 'Cousin Kate', 'Half-caste' or 'The Class Game'.

Sample analysis

'No Problem' and 'The Destruction of Sennacherib' use rhyme in different ways. Zephaniah's poem appears to be written in free verse, with lines of unequal length. However, the poem is made up of a series of quatrains. In the first section most lines contain three stressed syllables, with occasional variations, giving it a strong rhythm similar to that of a traditional ballad. Ballad form is also apparent in the *abcb* rhyme scheme. The rhyme helps to make the poem appear light-hearted despite its serious subject matter. Like the strong rhythm, it also reflects the poem's origin as a poem to be recited or read aloud, as traditional ballads were.

'The Destruction of Sennacherib' uses rhyming couplets, the regularity of which gives a feeling of certainty and strength. Like Zephaniah, Byron writes in quatrains, but here they are clearly set out as stanzas. Also, the lines are longer and more regular, with four stressed syllables to each one, although he does vary the number of unstressed syllables occasionally. Unlike Zephaniah, Byron does not use rhyme for comic effect but, like him, he uses it to convey a sense of confidence and pride.

Questions

QUICK TEST

1. How do the first four lines establish the speaker's identity?
2. What examples does he give of stereotypical views of black people?
3. What is the significance of the reference to Timbuktu?
4. How does the tone of the poem change in the final section?

EXAM PRACTICE

Using one or two of the highlighted quotations to learn, write a paragraph about how Zephaniah explores racism.

WHAT WERE THEY LIKE?
by Denise Levertov

1) Did the people of Viet Nam
   use lanterns of stone?
2) Did they hold ceremonies
   to reverence the opening of buds?
5 3) Were they inclined to quiet laughter?
4) Did they use bone and ivory,
   jade and silver, for ornament?
5) Had they an epic poem?
6) Did they distinguish between speech and singing?

10 1) Sir, their light hearts turned to stone.
   It is not remembered whether in gardens
   stone lanterns illumined pleasant ways.
2) Perhaps they gathered once to delight in blossom,
   but after their children were killed
15   there were no more buds.
3) Sir, laughter is bitter to the burned mouth.
4) A dream ago, perhaps. Ornament is for joy.
   All the bones were charred.
5) It is not remembered. Remember,
20   most were peasants; their life
   was in rice and bamboo.
   When peaceful clouds were reflected in the paddies
   and the water buffalo stepped surely along terraces,
   maybe fathers told their sons old tales.
25   When bombs smashed those mirrors
   there was time only to scream.
6) There is an echo yet
   Of their speech which was like a song.
   It was reported that their singing resembled
30   the flight of moths in moonlight.
   Who can say? It is silent now.

This poem is about...

the destruction of a country's culture and civilisation in war. It is specifically about the possible outcome of the **Vietnam War**.

How does the first part of the poem introduce its themes and ideas?

The poem starts with six questions. They are numbered and are not answered at this point, giving the impression of a questionnaire that has been submitted in writing. They might be asked by a journalist, an academic researcher or someone conducting a military or political enquiry. The title implies that the people either no longer exist or that their way of life has completely changed.

The first question tells the reader that the poem is about Vietnam. When the poem was written, America and other countries were heavily involved in that war, which had already gone on for over ten years and which was to carry on for many more. The use of the past tense suggests that the poet is imagining a time in the future, after the war. She is not optimistic about the outcome for the Vietnamese people and their culture.

The six questions are the kind that might be asked about an ancient, lost culture. Each one is based on an aspect of traditional Vietnamese culture. Taken together, they evoke a peaceful, gentle culture that valued the beauty of nature and art.

How does the poet explore effects of war in the first four answers?

The second part of the poem gives the answers to the questions. The language is polite and formal, with the use of 'Sir'. However, each answer emphasises the effects of the war on Vietnamese culture, something which the questioner has not asked about. Answer 1 uses the image of the 'stone lanterns' to express the effect of war on the people's spirits, punning on the light from the lantern to use 'light' in the sense of carefree or happy and using 'stone' as a metaphor for lack of feeling. The following two lines answer the question directly, saying that 'It is not remembered' but then giving detail that suggests the speaker does in fact remember. Answer 2 starts with a non-committal 'perhaps' before focusing on the effects of the war and associating children with the 'buds' of the blossoms. The death of the children destroys hope. The third answer begins with the polite 'Sir' but seems to upbraid 'Sir' for asking such a question in view of the circumstances, referring to the violence and horror of war from the victims' point of view. Their mouths may literally have been 'burned' by **napalm** and the bitterness they feel is both literal and metaphorical. Answer 4 suggests that the ideas of beauty and ornament are now a fantasy, having no place in post-war Vietnam. The speaker uses the word 'bone' (used in the question to denote the animal bones from which jewellery was made) to present a horrific image of the effects of the war. 'All the bones' includes people's bones. The passive verb 'were charred', describes the effects of the bombs dropped on civilians.

How are the themes developed in lines 19–26?

Question 5 is the shortest question but receives the longest response, appropriately as it is about an epic poem. The speaker repeats 'It is not remembered', but then tells the questioner what he should remember: that most of the people were 'peasants', whose lives would not be associated with the arts. The simplicity and harshness of their living is conveyed in the phrase 'rice and bamboo', referring to the staples of their existence. However, this is followed by two long lines which describe a kind of idyll, conveying the beauty of traditional life in the peaceful countryside. The poet uses 'f' and 's' sounds to soften the steady, slow-paced lines. The speaker concedes that in these conditions poetry and literature could have been created by the telling of 'old tales'. The last two lines shatter the peaceful atmosphere with another reference to violence. This time the speaker uses the active mood and refers overtly to bombing. 'When bombs smashed those mirrors' uses the idea of the water reflecting the clouds from line 22 to create an image of sudden violence and destruction. The metaphor of broken mirrors also has connotations of the people losing their ability to look at themselves and their lives. The line 'there was time only to scream' conveys the terror of the victims and the irrelevance of talk of poetry.

What is the effect of the final answer (lines 27–31)?

The answer to the last question is reflective and lyrical but leaves readers with the sense that, although the country is now peaceful, it is empty. There is only an 'echo' left of the 'speech which was like a song'. This could mean that the people's language has been destroyed along with other aspects of their culture or even that there is no-one left to speak it. The poet uses natural imagery to describe their singing: 'the flight of moths in moonlight' uses soft sounds and alliteration to create a sense of almost unearthly beauty. In this last answer, there is no reference to war or violence. The final line starts with a short rhetorical question. After the caesura created by the question mark, the speaker sums up the effects of the war with the simple sentence 'It is silent now'. This contrasts with the 'scream' of the previous answer and leaves the reader with a sense of sadness and finality.

How does the poem's form contribute to how meaning is conveyed?

The poem is written in free verse, divided into two stanzas of unequal length. The numbering of the questions and answers makes it visually striking – like an official document, perhaps a report or part of an academic thesis. It helps to create a calm, unemotional tone.

The lines are of unequal length and have no rhyme or regular rhythm. The punctuation and **syntax** are formal and add to the poem being an academic, almost scientific, text.

Additional context to consider

Levertov, although born and brought up in Britain, spent most of her life in America and is usually thought of as an American poet. During the 1950s and '60s she was a political activist and part of the anti-war movement in response to American involvement in Vietnam.

Written at the height of the war, this poem can be seen as a poem of protest against that war and war in general. It imagines a time after the war when the pre-war traditional Vietnamese culture would seem as distant as an ancient civilisation. It is now over forty years since the end of the Vietnam War. It might be interesting to reflect on to what extent Levertov was right in her pessimism about the country's future.

Poetic links

- Memories in 'The Prelude', 'Catrin' or 'Poppies'.
- The effects of war in 'Exposure', 'War Photographer' or 'The Destruction of Sennacherib'.
- Identity in 'Half-caste', 'No Problem', 'The Class Game' or 'Catrin'.
- Non-European cultures in 'No Problem', 'The Destruction of Sennacherib' or 'War Photographer'.

Sample analysis

Questions are important in both 'What Were They Like?' and 'Belfast Confetti'. Even the title of 'What Were They Like?' is a question. The use of the past tense implies that 'they' either no longer exist or have been radically changed. The question turns out not to be rhetorical but a genuine enquiry from one speaker to another. The questions that follow, in the style of a numbered questionnaire that might be used in an academic or official report, are looking for information. They start with 'Did they', 'Were they' and 'Had they', not 'Why' or 'How'. This helps to establish a calm, unemotional tone – a sense that we will be presented with facts, not opinions.

In contrast, Carson's questions are rhetorical. They arise from a frightening situation and have a feeling of panic. The first asks, 'Why can't I escape?'. This addresses the immediate, literal problem but also a deeper concern about why he and others are trapped in a long-standing conflict. The three successive questions of the last line, apparently asked by the soldiers, use the first person pronouns 'I' and 'my', suggesting he is also asking them of himself. He is questioning his identity, his past and future, and by implication the history and future of Belfast.

Questions

QUICK TEST
1. What impression might the unusual layout of the poem give a reader?
2. How does the poet use the image of blossom to convey a loss of hope?
3. Which two verbs, in the passive, describe the effects of bombing on the people?
4. To what does the metaphor 'mirrors' refer?

EXAM PRACTICE
Using one or two of the highlighted quotations to learn, write a paragraph exploring how Levertov presents the destruction of a culture.

How to Compare Poetry

How do I tackle a poetry comparison question?

On your question paper, in Section B Part 1, you will see three poems, one for each section of the poetry anthology. Look for the heading 'Conflict'. Under this heading, there will be one of the poems you have studied followed by a question. The question will ask you to choose one other poem from the *Conflict* anthology and compare it with the printed poem.

The exam board has stressed that, although you do not get separate marks for comparison, you are expected to meet the requirements of AO2 (analysis) and AO3 (context) (see pages 79–80) through the comparisons you make.

You do not have to give the two poems exactly equal coverage but if you only write about one poem, you cannot get a good mark. The same applies if your answer is unbalanced, meaning that you have spent little time on one of the poems.

There are different ways of doing comparison essays. Some candidates simply write about one poem and then about the other. This is not a comparison and will not attract good marks. It is acceptable to write about the first poem and then about the second, as long as you refer back to the first after each point you make. However, the examiners say that the best answers compare the two poems from the start of the answer, looking at different aspects of the poems and using details from them to explore similarities and differences.

As you will not be given a choice of question, you will have to revise all the poems in the anthology. When you decide which poem to compare with the given one, make your choice carefully. Think about the focus of the question and consider which of the other poems in the anthology might be suitable. If the question focuses on a very general theme, such as emotions or conflict, you could use any of the other poems. If, however, it is a narrower theme such as 'parents and children' or 'war', your choice is limited. (Look at the 'Poetic links' sections in this book for some ideas about themes that link various poems.) Having decided which poems you could use, choose a poem that gives you plenty of scope for identifying both similarities to and differences from the given poem. It is a good idea to choose a poem that you like and can write enthusiastically about: you are also more likely to remember a poem that you like.

In the exam you will only have a very short time to choose your poem and do a quick plan before you start to write. Therefore, it is important that you have practised comparing poems during your revision. Use the practice questions (pages 76–78) to revise by planning possible answers in greater detail than you would be able to in the exam. Have a look at this one:

1. Re-read *A Poison Tree*. Choose **one** other poem from the *Conflict* anthology. Compare how strong emotions are presented in the two poems.
    In your answer you should consider:

    • the poets' use of language, form and structure

    • the influence of the contexts in which the poems were written.

The focus of this question is quite broad. If you look at the list of poems in the anthology you will see that many of them could be used. 'A Poison Tree' is about anger. Poems with obvious similarities include 'Cousin Kate' and 'No Problem'. There is also a feeling of anger in 'Half-caste' and 'The Class Game'. 'The Destruction of Sennacherib' features the anger of God. Other poems feature different strong emotions: love in 'Poppies' and 'Catrin'; fear in 'The Prelude', 'Belfast Confetti' and to some extent in 'War Photographer' and 'What Were They Like?'. 'The Charge of the Light Brigade', 'Exposure' and 'The Man He Killed' do not feature people experiencing strong emotions, but it could be argued that the poets feel strongly about their subjects.

Think about various aspects of the poems that you could compare. You might want to draw up a table like the one below. (Remember that in the exam, you won't have time to make such a detailed plan. This is for revision purposes.)

	'A Poison Tree'	'Cousin Kate'
Title	Refers to the dominant image of the poem, symbolising the speaker's anger.	The name of the person who is causing the speaker's strong emotions.
Voice	First person – the speaker may be the poet or a persona.	First person – uses a persona (a rejected lover).
What happens in the poem	The speaker does not tell his enemy about his anger. Imagining it as a tree, he cultivates the tree until an apple grows on it. His enemy steals the apple and is poisoned by it.	The speaker has been seduced by a rich man and then rejected when he fell in love with and married her cousin. The speaker reveals she has something better than wealth – her son.
Themes (strong emotions)	Anger, how it can grow and its effect.	Sorrow, anger, bitterness, jealousy, shame and pride.
The poet's attitude	Blake is showing the effects of repressing emotion. The poison destroys the speaker as well as his foe.	The poet does not give her opinion but presents her persona's feelings in her own words.
Structure and form	A variation on ballad form – regular rhyming quatrains, mostly in (truncated) trochaic tetrameter.	Also a variation on ballad form – eight-line stanzas, each containing two regular quatrains, in alternating tetrameter and trimeter, mostly iambic.
Imagery	One extended metaphor of the poison tree.	Imagery of clothes and ornaments. Kate and the speaker both compared to birds.
Sounds	Sibilance used to show deceit.	Onomatopoeia to show emotion ('howl', 'moan'). Alliteration to show strength of love for her son.
Other language features	Repetition, anaphora. Simple vocabulary and syntax.	Repetition. Oxymoron to express mixed emotions.
Context	Early Romantic – interest in simple, traditional forms. Blake's concern with repression. Biblical reference.	Pre-Raphaelite – historic feel. Conventional morality and the results of transgressing. Position of women. Fairy-tale aspect.

You can see from the table that there are many points of comparison between the poems.

Use this table when revising other pairs of poems. (Bear in mind that not all the rows may be relevant to all the poems.)

You will have quite a short time to write your essay in the exam and the examiners do not expect you to be able to cover every possible valid point. However, if you have revised thoroughly, you should be able to cover a range of points effectively. Remember these must include analysis of structure and form, language and context. You should try to compare a few aspects of each of these. It is better to refer to aspects of context as you go along than to consider them separately.

How do I structure a poetry comparison essay?

Start your essay with a brief introduction. This should:

- tell the examiner which poems you are writing about
- make a statement that focuses on the question, relating it to both poems.

For example:

> The speakers in 'A Poison Tree' and 'Cousin Kate' both experience strong emotions. Blake focuses on anger, while Rossetti's persona undergoes a variety of strong, sometimes conflicting, feelings.

The opening sentence mentions both poems and the question, and points out a similarity between them. Still focusing on the question, the second sentence points out a difference between the themes of the poems. Note that the poets are referred to by their surnames. You can also refer to the poet simply as 'the poet'.

If you decide to write about one poem and then the other, remember to spend roughly 15 minutes on each. Make sure that when you are writing about the second poem you keep referring back to the first. You can use phrases like:

- 'Unlike Blake...'
- 'Rossetti, like Blake, uses...'
- 'In comparison...'
- 'Similarly...'.

However, it is better to look at the two poems together. The easiest way of doing this is to alternate your paragraphs between the poems, although there may be times when you want to mention both in the same paragraph. Here is a way of approaching the comparison:

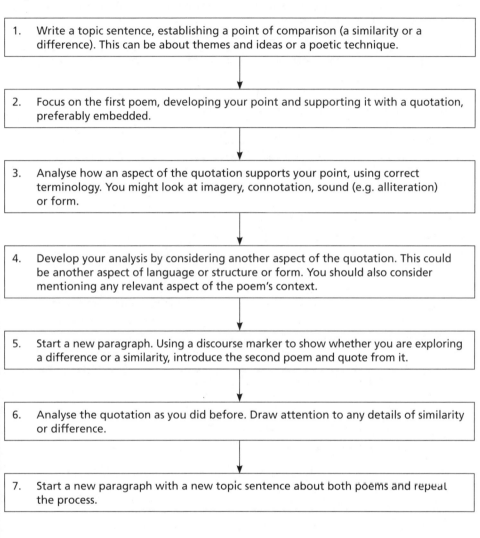

1. Write a topic sentence, establishing a point of comparison (a similarity or a difference). This can be about themes and ideas or a poetic technique.

2. Focus on the first poem, developing your point and supporting it with a quotation, preferably embedded.

3. Analyse how an aspect of the quotation supports your point, using correct terminology. You might look at imagery, connotation, sound (e.g. alliteration) or form.

4. Develop your analysis by considering another aspect of the quotation. This could be another aspect of language or structure or form. You should also consider mentioning any relevant aspect of the poem's context.

5. Start a new paragraph. Using a discourse marker to show whether you are exploring a difference or a similarity, introduce the second poem and quote from it.

6. Analyse the quotation as you did before. Draw attention to any details of similarity or difference.

7. Start a new paragraph with a new topic sentence about both poems and repeat the process.

What should a comparison look like?

If you look back at the 'Sample analysis' sections on pages 7–69, you will get a good idea of the sort of comparisons you can make and how to make them.

Here is part of a comparison essay answering the question on page 70. Look at how it follows the flow chart on page 73.

Both poems end with the speakers expressing joy at their triumph, or potential triumph, over their enemies.[1] Blake states quite simply that he is 'glad' to 'see/My foe outstretch'd beneath the tree.'[2] The straightforward single-syllable adjective 'glad' does not convey a strongly held emotion but this use of understatement helps to create an unsettling effect on the reader. It is a calm and emotionless reaction to having killed someone.[3] He refers, for the third time, to 'my foe'. This reminds us that he has given no reason for his anger and has not identified the 'foe' in any way. This makes both the speaker and his foe into 'everyman' figures, the poem being a **fable** about what would happen to anyone who repressed their anger. The poem ends with the powerful image of the speaker's enemy lying dead 'beneath the tree', leaving the reader with a final disturbing picture of the symbol of the speaker's anger and repression towering triumphantly over his enemy.[4]

The speaker in 'Cousin Kate' also leaves us contemplating a symbol of her emotional state, her 'fair-haired son'.[5] His fair hair recalls her own 'flaxen hair', used in the first stanza to denote the beauty which attracted the 'lord' to her. Her son is revealed as the 'gift' that is more valuable than anything Kate has received from the lord. In this he represents a victory over her rival. The apparently contradictory **abstract nouns** 'my shame, my pride' show how complex the persona's emotions are, unlike the straightforward and unexplained 'wrath' of Blake's speaker. This suggests that she feels the 'shame' that society would expect from her but also 'pride', not just in him personally but in the 'shameful' love he represents. His existence represents a triumph over Kate but, unlike that of Blake's speaker, her triumph may not yet be complete. The final line hints at a possibility that he might one day gain his father's 'coronet', the symbol of his wealth and power.[6]

[1] The topic sentence clearly establishes the point of comparison: the theme of presenting triumph over an enemy.

[2] Explores how Blake expresses his speaker's triumph, with a relevant quotation.

[3] A detail of language is analysed, in this case a single word and its connotations. Relevant subject terminology is used (syllable, adjective, understatement).

[4] Explores two further details. Uses 'foe' to refer to the poem's structure and use of repetition, before focusing on the tree as a symbol. Relevant terminology is used. Context is considered in the references to the poem as a fable and Blake's concern with repression.

5   Moves onto 'Cousin Kate'. The discourse marker 'also' shows that a similarity is being considered at the beginning.

6   Several quotations are analysed, all short and embedded. Language and imagery are analysed using appropriate terminology. Structure and form are also considered (stanza, persona). Context ('society') is briefly mentioned. Notice that 'A Poison Tree' is referred to twice in this paragraph, pointing out differences between the poems.

Questions

QUICK TEST

1. How many poems will you write about in the exam?

2. How should you decide which poem to choose?

3. Is it better to write half your answer on one poem and the other half on the other poem, or to compare them throughout the essay?

4. What should you do in your topic sentence? ·

EXAM PRACTICE

Look again at the table on page 71, the flow chart on page 73 and the example analysis on page 74. Now write another section of analysis comparing how strong emotions are presented in 'A Poison Tree' and 'Cousin Kate'.

1. Re-read *A Poison Tree*. Choose **one** other poem from the *Conflict* anthology.

    Compare how strong emotions are presented in the two poems.

    In your answer you should consider:
    - the poets' use of language, form and structure
    - the influence of the contexts in which the poems were written.

2. Re-read *The Destruction of Sennacherib*. Choose **one** other poem from the *Conflict* anthology.

    Compare how war is presented in the two poems.

    In your answer you should consider:
    - the poets' use of language, form and structure
    - the influence of the contexts in which the poems were written.

3. Re-read the extract from *The Prelude*. Choose **one** other poem from the *Conflict* anthology.

    Compare how childhood is presented in the two poems.

    In your answer you should consider:
    - the poets' use of language, form and structure
    - the influence of the contexts in which the poems were written.

4. Re-read *The Man He Killed*. Choose **one** other poem from the *Conflict* anthology.

    Compare how acts of violence are presented in the two poems.

    In your answer you should consider:
    - the poets' use of language, form and structure
    - the influence of the contexts in which the poems were written.

5. Re-read *Cousin Kate.* Choose **one** other poem from the *Conflict* anthology.

    Compare how suffering is presented in the two poems.

    In your answer you should consider:
    - the poets' use of language, form and structure
    - the influence of the contexts in which the poems were written.

6. Re-read *Half-caste*. Choose **one** other poem from the *Conflict* anthology.

    Compare how a sense of being different is presented in the two poems.

    In your answer you should consider:
    - the poets' use of language, form and structure
    - the influence of the contexts in which the poems were written.

7. Re-read *Exposure*. Choose **one** other poem from the *Conflict* anthology.

   Compare how death is presented in the two poems.

   In your answer you should consider:
   - the poets' use of language, form and structure
   - the influence of the contexts in which the poems were written.

8. Re-read *The Charge of the Light Brigade*. Choose **one** other poem from the *Conflict* anthology.

   Compare how soldiers are presented in the two poems.

   In your answer you should consider:
   - the poets' use of language, form and structure
   - the influence of the contexts in which the poems were written.

9. Re-read *Catrin*. Choose **one** other poem from the *Conflict* anthology.

   Compare how life-changing experiences are presented in the two poems.

   In your answer you should consider:
   - the poets' use of language, form and structure
   - the influence of the contexts in which the poems were written.

10. Re-read *War Photographer*. Choose **one** other poem from the *Conflict* anthology.

    Compare how morality is presented in the two poems.

    In your answer you should consider:
    - the poets' use of language, form and structure
    - the influence of the contexts in which the poems were written.

11. Re-read *Belfast Confetti*. Choose **one** other poem from the *Conflict* anthology.

    Compare how the experience of being attacked is presented in the two poems.

    In your answer you should consider:
    - the poets' use of language, form and structure
    - the influence of the contexts in which the poems were written.

12. Re-read *The Class Game*. Choose **one** other poem from the *Conflict* anthology.

    Compare how pride is presented in the two poems.

    In your answer you should consider:
    - the poets' use of language, form and structure
    - the influence of the contexts in which the poems were written.

13. Re-read *Poppies*. Choose **one** other poem from the *Conflict* anthology.

    Compare how memories are presented in the two poems.

    In your answer you should consider:
    - the poets' use of language, form and structure
    - the influence of the contexts in which the poems were written.

14. Re-read *No Problem*. Choose **one** other poem from the *Conflict* anthology.

    Compare how power is presented in the two poems.

    In your answer you should consider:
    • the poets' use of language, form and structure
    • the influence of the contexts in which the poems were written.

15. Re-read *What Were They Like?* Choose **one** other poem from the *Conflict* anthology.

    Compare how cultural identity is presented in the two poems.

    In your answer you should consider:
    • the poets' use of language, form and structure
    • the influence of the contexts in which the poems were written.

16. Re-read *A Poison Tree*. Choose **one** other poem from the *Conflict* anthology.

    Compare how symbols are used in the two poems.

    In your answer you should consider:
    • the poets' use of language, form and structure
    • the influence of the contexts in which the poems were written.

17. Re-read *Cousin Kate*. Choose **one** other poem from the *Conflict* anthology.

    Compare the use of the first-person narrator in the two poems.

    In your answer you should consider:
    • the poets' use of language, form and structure
    • the influence of the contexts in which the poems were written.

18. Re-read *Catrin*. Choose **one** other poem from the *Conflict* anthology.

    Compare how women are presented in the two poems.

    In your answer you should consider:
    • the poets' use of language, form and structure
    • the influence of the contexts in which the poems were written.

19. Re-read *The Man He Killed*. Choose **one** other poem from the *Conflict* anthology.

    Compare how enemies are presented in the two poems.

    In your answer you should consider:
    • the poets' use of language, form and structure
    • the influence of the contexts in which the poems were written.

20. Re-read the extract from *The Prelude*. Choose **one** other poem from the *Conflict* anthology.

    Compare how nature is presented in the two poems.

    In your answer you should consider:
    • the poets' use of language, form and structure
    • the influence of the contexts in which the poems were written.

Tips

- You will be given one question on the *Conflict* anthology. There are also questions on the *Love and Relationships* and *Time and Place* anthologies. If you have studied more than one anthology, you can choose which question to answer. Otherwise, stick to *Conflict*.

- There will be a poem from the *Conflict* anthology reproduced in full and followed by a question which asks you to choose another poem from the *Conflict* anthology and to compare the two.

- It is essential that you write about two poems. If you do not, you cannot get a high mark.

- The question will include two bullet points to remind you to focus on the assessment objectives. One of these bullet points tells you to consider the poets' use of language, form and structure. The other tells you to consider the contexts in which the poems were written.

- Make sure you know what the question is asking you and underline key words.

- You should spend about 35 minutes on this question. Allow up to five minutes to plan your answer. This will help you to structure your essay.

- All your paragraphs should contain a clear idea, at least one quotation or close reference to the text, and analysis of how one or both poets convey this idea.

- You should try to link your comments to the contexts of the poems.

- Your paragraphs should be linked using discourse markers/connectives.

- It can help, after writing each paragraph, to quickly re-read the question in order to keep you focused on the task.

- Keep your writing concise and to the point. If you waste time 'waffling' you will not be able to include the full range of analysis that the mark scheme requires.

- Remember what the mark scheme is asking you to do.

Important

You **cannot** gain a good mark (the 'middle' level in the tables on page 80) if you only write about one poem.

Compare two poems

Comparison is an essential part of this question. It is not marked separately and does not come under a single Assessment Objective. You must answer the question you have been given and address both AO2 and AO3 through comparison.

Lower marks level	Middle marks level	Upper marks level
There are some comparisons and contrasts. Obvious similarities and/or differences have been pointed out, supported by some references to the poems.	The answer compares and contrasts a range of points and clearly considers some similarities and differences between the poems, supported by relevant examples.	The answer compares and contrasts the two poems effectively. It considers a varied range of similarities and/or differences between the poems, supported throughout by relevant examples from both poems.

The assessment objectives that relate to the poetry comparison question are as follows:

AO2: Analyse the effects of the poets' use of language, form and structure. (15 marks)

You need to compare how the two poets use specific words, language techniques, poetic forms, including metre, and the structure of their poems to get their ideas and feelings across.

Lower marks level	Middle marks level	Upper marks level
There is some comment on form and structure. Some awareness of the poets' use of language is shown but it is underdeveloped. There is limited use of relevant subject terminology.	There is a sound understanding of form and structure, linked to their effect on the reader. There is a clear awareness, supported by sound examples, of the poets' use of language and its effect on the reader. Relevant subject terminology is used to support the answer.	There is a perceptive and sustained understanding of form and structure and their effect on the reader. There is an effective evaluation of the poets' use of language and its effect on the reader. Relevant subject terminology is used accurately to develop ideas.

AO3: Understand the relationship between the poems and their contexts. (5 marks)

You need to show that you understand how the meanings of the poems and the ways they are received have been affected by the social, historical and literary contexts in which they were written.

Lower marks level	Middle marks level	Upper marks level
There is some awareness of relevant context and some comment on the relationship between the poems and their context.	There is sound, clear comment on relevant context and the relationship between the poems and their context.	There is sustained, convincing comment on relevant context and detailed awareness of the relationship between poems and context.

Planning a Poetry Response

How will the exam question be worded?

A typical poetry comparison question in your exam will look like this:

Re-read *The Man He Killed*. Choose **one** other poem from the *Conflict* anthology.

Compare how the experience of war is presented in the two poems.

In your answer you should consider:

- the poets' use of language, form and structure
- the influence of the contexts in which the poems were written.

How do I work out what to do?

The focus of the question is clear: war and how people experience it.

'Compare' and 'how' are key words in this and any other question you might be given.

'Compare' reminds you that you are writing about the two poems together and that you should make a number of structured and well-developed comparisons about the poets' depiction of the experience of war.

'How' tells you that you should analyse different ways in which the poets present these ideas. The first bullet point reminds you that you should write about language, form and structure, so ensure that all these elements are covered at some point in your answer.

You are expected to analyse details of the poems. The first poem is re-printed for you but you still need to quote from it. Use short quotations to illustrate your points and make sure you analyse aspects of language, form and structure. You should have learned quotations from the other poems in the anthology – if not whole poems – so you should be able to remember enough relevant material to use in the exam. If you cannot remember quotations, make clear references to specific parts of the poem.

The second bullet point reminds you that you must comment on the 'contexts' in which the poems were written. These contexts can include relevant ideas about the poets' lives and opinions, events that inspired the poems, social and historical context, and literary traditions and movements.

How can I plan my essay?

You have approximately **35 minutes** to write your answer. This isn't very long but it will help if you spend up to five minutes writing a quick plan. This will help you to focus your thoughts and produce a well-structured essay.

The first thing you need to do is to pick your second poem. Make sure it suits the question. The question on page 81 limits your choice because not all the poems are concerned with the experience of war.

Try to come up with at least three areas for comparison. These can be similarities and/or differences. It may also help to jot down some appropriate quotations that you have learned from the second poem. For more detailed advice about planning a comparison essay, look back at pages 70–74, but bear in mind that the advice given there is for revision purposes. You will **not** have time to produce a detailed table of comparisons in the exam itself.

You can plan in whatever way you find most useful. Some people like to make a list of points and then number them to give a logical order. Others use spider diagrams. Look at this example:

The experience of war

'The Man He Killed'   'What Were They Like?'

Voice/point of view
- Persona: Country man – served as a soldier – killed a man – tries to work out why – lack of emotion: 'Because he was my foe', 'Just so: my foe of course he was;'
- Two voices – one academic/reporter, removed from action – the other more knowledgeable but not personally involved – formal but uses figurative imagery: 'Sir, their light hearts turned to stone'

Structure
- Ballad – regular quatrains – speech marks
- Free verse – questions and answers – uneven stanza and line length

Victims
- Individual – close combat – speaker imagines him as being like himself: 'I shot at him as he at me', 'just as I'
- Whole civilisation – bombing – civilian casualties – emphasis on suffering: 'All the bones were charred'; 'there was time only to scream'

War and peace
- Reference to normal times as contrast: 'By some old ancient inn,/ We should have sat us down'
- Description of aftermath compared to pre-war normality: 'When peaceful clouds were reflected in the paddies'

Attitudes to war
- Real war but could be any war – no sense of reason – pointless: 'You'd treat if met where any bar is', 'quaint and curious'
- Real war – specific – sense of sadness at the scale of destruction – warning about future? 'the flight of moths in moonlight'

Summary

- Make sure you know what the focus of the question is.
- Remember to compare the two poems.
- Remember to analyse how the poets use language, form and structure to convey their ideas.
- Remember to relate the poems to their contexts.

Questions

QUICK TEST

1. What key elements of the poems should you cover in your answer?
2. What are the benefits of doing a quick plan?
3. What is the first thing you should do when planning your answer?

EXAM PRACTICE

Plan a response to the following exam question:

Re-read *Belfast Confetti*. Choose **one** other poem from the *Conflict* anthology. Compare how vulnerability is presented in the two poems.

In your answer you should consider:

- the poets' use of language, form and structure
- the influence of the contexts in which the poems were written.

Re-read *The Man He Killed*. Choose **one** other poem from the *Conflict* anthology.

Compare how the experience of war is presented in the two poems.

In your answer you should consider:

- the poets' use of language, form and structure
- the influence of the contexts in which the poems were written.   [20 marks]

'The Man He Killed' and 'What Were They Like?' are both about war.[1] 'The Man He Killed' is about a soldier who has killed another man. He tries to explain why he killed him. He says it was 'because he was my foe', meaning his enemy. He was just told he was his enemy and he accepts it as 'Just so'. He shows no emotion but talking about it makes him think more about it and the way the lines are broken up shows he has doubts.[2]

'What Were They Like?' has two speakers.[3] The first asks questions. He might be a reporter who is trying to find out what it was like in Vietnam before the war. The second speaker answers the questions. He is polite and formal, saying 'Sir'. But he shows some emotion, especially sadness. The line 'their light hearts turned to stone' shows he is not involved because he uses 'their' but the metaphor 'light' tells the reader about the change that has come over them.[4]

'The Man He Killed' is very traditional and is in five equal stanzas, all rhyming and with the same metre. This shows he is calm most of the time. 'What Were They Like?' is more modern and has lines of different lengths. The way it is set out with numbered questions and answers is very unusual.[5]

'The Man He Killed' is about one person and his experience but 'What Were They Like?' is about a whole country's experience.[6] The speaker says 'I shot at him as he at me' which tells us what it is like to fight hand-to-hand, and 'as he at me' and 'just as I' shows they are both the same. He uses ordinary language as if he is having a chat. He does not describe any of the horror of war.[7]

In contrast, Levertov uses metaphors to show how horrible war is for the victims.[8] She compares the children to 'buds' that could not grow into flowers. She uses verbs like 'charred' and 'burned' to show suffering. After the bombs were dropped 'there was time only to scream'. This contrasts with the time before the war. Then people led a peaceful life working in the 'paddies'. The poet uses 'peaceful clouds' to show this. This is pathetic fallacy.[9]

The man in 'The Man He Killed' also led a quiet life before the war but he was unemployed, which is why he enlisted. He thinks about how it would have been for him and the man he killed if they had met in peacetime. He imagines they would go to an 'old ancient inn', which is a typical English scene. For the speaker, life has gone back to normal, unlike in the other poem.[10]

Both poems are about real wars. 'The Man He Killed' is about the Boer War but it does not say so, so it could be what any soldier experienced. 'What Were They Like?' is about the Vietnam War. This was in the 1960s. Civilians were bombed and the poet thinks their civilisation has been destroyed.[11] The speaker remembers how beautiful their culture was. She says their language was like 'moths in moonlight'. The alliteration stresses how quiet and gentle it was and makes you feel sad about the war. Hardy's attitude to war is that it is 'quaint and curious'. This conveys the idea that there is no reason for war.[12]

1   A clear introduction that tells us which two poems are being used but it is vague and would be better if something was said here about how they differ.

2   Clear awareness of the use of language and its effects but not much analysis. The reference to structure is more analytical.

3   This is not clearly linked to the previous paragraph as a point of contrast.

4   Begins to analyse the use of language, using relevant terminology.

5   Reasonable attempt at comparing the poems' structures and form but it is not linked to the rest of the essay. There is, however, clear consideration of differences and relevant terminology.

6   This paragraph starts with a clear topic sentence, comparing the poems.

7   Clear reference to the effect of the poet's use of language, using relevant examples from the text.

8   Topic sentence effectively connected to the previous paragraph, clearly describing an important difference between the poems and using relevant terminology.

9   Uses several very short quotations from the text effectively. There could be more analysis of the language but some relevant terminology is used. The writer smoothly moves to the next point.

10   Effective comparison of the two poems. Comparison has become much better towards the end of the essay. Relevant quotation but a lack of analysis.

11   Sound comment on context, relating it to the poems. More references to context, integrated into the answer, could have been made earlier.

12   Relevant quotations with some analysis but the conclusion of the essay could be stronger and more focused on comparison.

> ## Question
>
> EXAM PRACTICE
> Choose two paragraphs from this essay. Read them through a few times. Then try to improve them. You might:
> * Improve the clarity of expression and the sophistication of the language.
> * Replace a reference with a quotation or use a more relevant quotation.
> * Give more detailed analysis.
> * Use subject terminology more effectively.
> * Link references to context to your analysis more effectively.

A proportion of the best top-band answers will be awarded grade 8 or 9. To achieve this your essay should be sophisticated, fluent and nuanced, displaying flair and originality.

Re-read *The Man He Killed*. Choose **one** other poem from the *Conflict* anthology.

Compare how the experience of war is presented in the two poems.

In your answer you should consider:

- the poets' use of language, form and structure
- the influence of the contexts in which the poems were written. [20 marks]

'The Man He Killed' and 'What Were They Like?' are both about how people experience war but are written from different perspectives.[1] Hardy's persona is an ordinary working man who served as a soldier. He explains that he killed another man 'Because he was my foe'. He uses two single-syllable words 'Just so' to reinforce the simplicity of the idea and his acceptance of it. This is followed by a colon, suggesting an explanation might follow. Instead, he says 'my foe of course he was', suggesting their enmity is a matter of fact needing no explanation. The next line is also broken by a caesura and ends with a conjunction, 'although'. The enjambment between this and the fourth stanza, as well as the use of caesura, reflects his thought process and shows him starting to have doubts about the situation.[2] However, he is unemotional, his control reflected in the regularity of the quatrains. Hardy's structure, a variation on ballad form, suits both subject matter and speaker, as traditional ballads told dramatic stories in simple forms.[3]

Levertov's structure is neither traditional nor regular.[4] While her 'question and answer' format distances us from the experience of war, her use of free verse allows emotions to break out as the second speaker relates the experience of the Vietnamese people.[5] Like Hardy's persona, the speakers are looking back on the past. The questioner might be a reporter or an academic. His tone is formal, as is that of the second speaker, who addresses him politely as 'Sir'. However, while answering the questions, which are about life before the war, this speaker gradually introduces the subject of the war. In his first answer he picks up on the phrase 'lanterns of stone' and turns it into a metaphor. The phrase 'their light hearts turned to stone' suggests the psychological effects of war on the people without overtly mentioning the war.[6]

'What Were They Like?' reflects on a whole country's experience of war. Levertov uses images taken from Vietnamese culture to show the horror of the war. She uses the tradition of celebrating spring as a metaphor for the death of children, who are compared to 'buds' that could not open. The question about laughter evokes the response that the people's mouths were 'burned', while the bones referred to in question 4 become the 'charred' bones of the victims, the passive verbs emphasising their suffering and referencing the effects of napalm.[7]

In contrast, 'The Man He Killed' does not dwell on the details of killing and suffering. The speaker describes the experience of 'hand-to-hand fighting' in simple terms devoid of emotion: 'I shot at him as he at me'. This sentence, made up of single-syllable words, encapsulates the speaker's theme: he and the man he killed are the same.

He regrets that they had to be enemies and not friends, who might have drunk together in an 'old ancient inn'. The tautology of this phrase introduces a gently humorous tone, also conveying the homeliness of a typically English scene. There is a sense that, after war, life goes back to normal for the survivors.[8]

Levertov also contrasts war with peace. She too pictures an idyllic way of life. In the fifth answer, two long lines slow down the pace of the poem, describing the gentle pace of life before the war. She uses pathetic fallacy in 'peaceful clouds' to reflect rural life, adding to the gentle tone by using soft 'f' and 's' sounds. The phrase 'stepped surely along terraces' conveys a sense of the security and calmness of a traditional way of life before it is destroyed by bombs.[9] 'What Were They Like?' describes how war can completely destroy a civilisation. Unlike Hardy's soldier, the Vietnamese people do not return to normality.[10]

This difference is partly due to the way in which war has changed. 'The Man He Killed' is about the experience of ordinary soldiers. 'What Were They Like?', on the other hand, focuses entirely on civilians, reflecting the massive civilian casualties of the Vietnam War and the poet's fear that a whole civilisation was being destroyed.[11] The final line consists of a question and a simple answer, 'It is silent now'. This leaves the reader with an image of utter destruction and a feeling of great sadness. There is nothing positive about the experience of war. Hardy expresses a similar attitude in a very different way. The speaker tells us that war is 'quaint and curious', using understatement to make it look ridiculous as well as without reason. Both poems end with a sense of the pointlessness of war.[12]

[1] Clear introduction that tells us which two poems are being used and gives a sense of how they differ.

[2] Analysis of the effects of language and structure, closely referring to the text and using relevant subject terminology.

[3] Comment on context related to the poem's form.

[4] The topic sentence is clearly linked to the previous paragraph. Note that it is done without using an obvious 'comparing word'.

[5] Develops the point by discussing the effect of the poet's use of form and structure, using accurate terminology.

[6] Sustained analysis of both language and form, using relevant quotations and appropriate terminology. Comparison of the poems is clear.

[7] Introduces a new topic discussing the effects of the language and integrating a reference to context.

[8] Starts with a clear point of comparison and goes on to analyse the effects of the poet's use of language using accurate terminology.

[9] Starts with a clear point of similarity. Evaluates the poet's use of language and its effects.

[10] The paragraph ends with a point of difference between the poems, leading smoothly into the final paragraph.

[11] Considers relevant context, showing understanding of how it relates to the themes of the poems.

[12] Ends effectively by comparing the poems. The essay has covered a wide range of similarities and differences; analysed and evaluated the poets' use of form, structure and language; used accurate and relevant terminology; and commented effectively on relevant aspects of context.

Question

EXAM PRACTICE

Using the plan you have already prepared (page 83), spend 35 minutes writing an answer to the exam question:

Re-read *Belfast Confetti*. Choose **one** other poem from the *Conflict* anthology.

Compare how vulnerability is presented in the two poems.

In your answer you should consider:

- the poets' use of language, form and structure
- the influence of the contexts in which the poems were written.   [20 marks]

Glossary

Glossary of literary and linguistic terms

Abstract noun – a noun which denotes an idea or feeling, rather than an object

Active verb – when the subject performs the action, e.g. 'the dog bit the boy'

Alliteration – repetition of a consonant sound in two or more words, especially at the beginning of each word

Ambiguity (adj. ambiguous) – having more than one meaning

Anaphora – the repetition of a word or phrase at intervals, usually at the beginning of a line or sentence

Anecdote – a short narrative account, often used to reinforce a point being made

Anti-climax – a lapse from intensity to triviality

Antithesis – the opposite

Assonance – repetition of vowel sounds within words

Autobiographical – about the writer's life

Ballad – a form of poetry that tells a story, usually in quatrains with a regular rhythm and rhyme scheme

Caesura – a pause in a line of poetry, usually indicated by a punctuation mark

Chronological order – in order of time, starting with the earliest event

Cliché – an overused word, phrase or idea

Colloquial – conversational or chatty

Conjunction – a word used to join together two words or phrases, showing the relationship between them

Connotation – a meaning or association suggested by a word or phrase

Determiner – a short word that comes before a noun and helps to define it, including the definite article ('the') and the indefinite article ('a')

Dialect – words or phrases particular to a regional variety of English

Diction – the choice of words or phrases used

Discourse marker – a word or phrase that connects sentences or paragraphs

Dramatic monologue – a poem in which the poet adopts a persona to speak to the reader or audience

End stop – to use punctuation to indicate a pause at the end of a line of poetry

Enjambment – when lines are not end-stopped with a punctuation mark but the sense runs on between lines or stanzas

Epiphany – a moment of revelation or insight

Eponymous – adjective applied to the person after whom something is named

Extended metaphor – a metaphor that is developed at some length

Fable – a story with a moral

Figurative imagery – the use of an image of one thing to tell us about another, including metaphor, simile, personification, pathetic fallacy

First person – Singular – 'I' (subject), 'me' (object); Plural – 'we' (subject)', 'us' (object).

Folk ballad – a traditional ballad, usually passed down by word of mouth

Foreshadow – to suggest something that will happen later

Half-rhyme (also slant rhyme or pararhyme) – an imperfect rhyme in which the final consonants of a line agree but the vowels do not

Idyll (adj. idyllic) – a description of an idealised version of a peaceful or picturesque life

Imagery – the use of words to paint pictures in readers' minds

Imperative – a form of verb used for a command or order

Imply – to suggest something that is not openly stated

In media res – in the middle of the action

Irony – when words are used to imply an opposite meaning

Juxtaposition (verb juxtapose) – the placing of two words or phrases next to each other. The use of the term does not necessarily imply opposition or contrast

Lexical field – words or phrases relating to a particular subject

Literal imagery – the use of description of actual things to convey mood or atmosphere

Lyric poetry – short poems expressing personal feelings

Metaphor – an image created by writing about something as if it were something else

Mixed metaphor – when two metaphors are applied to one thing, the result often being illogical or ridiculous

Modal verb – a verb that shows the mood or state of another verb (e.g. 'could' or 'might')

Motif – an idea or image that is repeated at intervals in a text

Narrative poem – a poem, usually a long one, that tells a story

Onomatopoeia – the use of a word that sounds like the thing it describes

Oxymoron – two contradictory words placed together

Paradox – a self-contradictory statement or expression

Parallel phrasing/parallelism – repetition of the structure and some of the words in successive sentences or clauses

Passive verb – when the subject has something done to him or her, e.g. 'the boy was bitten by the dog'

Pathetic fallacy – either a form of personification, giving nature human qualities, or the use of description of surroundings to reflect a character's mood

Performance poet – a poet who recites or reads poetry aloud to audiences

Persona – a fictional voice adopted by a poet using the first person

Personification – when an inanimate object or idea is given human qualities

Plosive – an explosive sound such as 'b' or 'p'.

Proper noun – a noun that names an individual person or thing, such as a place or time; starts with a capital letter

Quatrain – a set of four lines of verse

Refrain – a repeated line or lines, usually at the end of a stanza

Rhetorical question – a question that does not require an answer

Rhyme – the use of words with the same ending to make patterns, usually at the ends of lines. If used within lines, referred to as 'internal rhyme'

Rhyming couplet – two successive lines that rhyme

Rhythm – the beat of the writing

Romanticism (adj. Romantic) – a literary movement of the early 19th century that focused on the freedom of individual expression, associated with intense personal feelings, a love of nature and the use of simple traditional forms

Second person – 'you' (both singular and plural)

Sibilance – the repetition of 's' sounds

Simile – a comparison of one thing to another using 'like' or 'as'

Slang – informal language, often regional and/ or changing quickly

Standard English – the variety of English generally accepted as the correct form for writing and formal speech

Stanza – a section of a poem, often called a verse. Usually, stanzas should be of equal length and regular. If not, especially in free verse, they are 'verse paragraphs'. However, it is acceptable to refer to these as stanzas

Stereotype – a person or thing that conforms to a generally accepted type. Usually used in a negative way

Syllable – a unit of pronunciation

Symbol – an object that represents something like an idea or emotion

Syntax – grammatical arrangement of words

Tautology – repetition of the same thing using different words

Tercet – a three-line stanza or set of lines

Triplet – a set of three lines, words or phrases

Vocabulary – words used

Metre

Metre is the pattern of stressed and unstressed syllables in verse. It is a way of describing a poem's rhythm.

A metrical foot is a unit of metre based on a small number of syllables, normally including one which is stressed. The types of foot you will come across are:

- Iamb – an unstressed syllable followed by a stressed syllable. This is the most commonly used foot. You will find it in 'The Prelude', 'A Poison Tree', 'Exposure', 'The Man He Killed', 'Cousin Kate' and 'No Problem'.
- Trochee – a stressed syllable followed by an unstressed syllable. See 'A Poison Tree', 'Exposure' and 'No Problem'.
- Spondee – two stressed syllables. Used rarely, for effect.
- Dactyl – a stressed syllable followed by two unstressed syllables. See 'The Charge of the Light Brigade'.
- Anapaest – two unstressed syllables followed by a stressed syllable. See 'The Destruction of Sennacherib'.

These terms are combined with words that describe the number of feet in a line to describe the line's structure.

- A line that consists of five iambs will, therefore, be called an **iambic pentameter**. 'The Prelude' is written in iambic pentameter.
- A **dimeter** contains two feet. Tennyson uses dactylic dimeter.
- A **trimeter** has three feet. Hardy and Rossetti use iambic trimeter.
- A **tetrameter** has four feet. Hardy and Rossetti also use iambic tetrameter. Blake uses both iambic and trochaic tetrameter. Byron uses anapaestic tetrameter.
- A **pentameter** has five feet. Wordsworth uses iambic pentameter.
- A **hexameter** has six feet. Owen uses hexameter, mostly iambic.

Many poems are regular, meaning that they use the same metre consistently in a pattern. However, you should look for times when poems that are basically regular do something different, for example using a trochee or spondee rather than an iamb; think about why the poets have done it. (See 'The Charge of the Light Brigade' and 'The Destruction of Sennacherib'.)

Most older poems also have a regular rhyme scheme. **Blank verse** is poetry that has a regular metre but does not rhyme.

Poetry that does not have either a regular metre or a regular rhyme scheme is called **free verse.** Most (but not all) modern poetry is written in free verse.

Remember, when writing about metre, it is not enough just to 'spot' the poet's technique. You must consider the effect of that technique.

General Glossary

Assyria – an ancient empire in the Middle East, centred on the present-day Syria and Iraq but at times covering much more territory

Boer Wars – (1880–1881 and 1889–1902) the name given to the South African wars fought between the British and the Boers (Dutch settlers) of South Africa

Colony (adj. colonial) – a settlement or conquered territory ruled by another nation

Conflate – combine

Crimean War – a war fought between the Russian Empire and an alliance of Britain, France, the Ottoman Empire and Sardinia from 1853 to 1856, originally about influence in the Holy Land. The alliance won but about 900,000 soldiers were killed

Derogatory – insulting

Ethnicity – racial origin and/or cultural identity

Existential – relating to existence (being)

Gamekeeper – a person employed by a landowner to look after animals bred for shooting

Incongruous – out of place

Innocuous – harmless

Judah – an ancient kingdom, whose capital was Jerusalem, in what is now the southern part of Israel

Minotaur – a mythical creature, half-man and half-bull, kept by King Minos in the labyrinth in Crete

Mystic – someone who tries to get close to God through contemplation and prayer.

Napalm – chemical used in bombs, especially during the Vietnam War

Nostalgia (adj. nostalgic) – yearning for the past

Nurture – to care for and help to grow

Objectify – to treat as an object

Omnipotence – all-knowing

Oppression – treating people harshly in order to control them

Ottoman Empire – (1299–1923) an empire ruled by Turkey, which at its height included much of Asia, eastern Europe and north Africa

Patronise – to treat as inferior

Penultimate – second to last

Poacher – someone who illegally hunts or traps animals

Poet laureate – the country's official poet, appointed by the monarch and expected to write about national events

Pre-Raphaelite – a group of English artists and writers in the late 19th century who rejected conventional academic styles and looked back to the Middle Ages for inspiration

Privilege – advantage

Salient – a part of the defences that protrudes into enemy territory

Seven deadly sins – in Christian tradition, seven behaviours that lead to immorality (pride, greed, lust, envy, gluttony, wrath and sloth)

Truce – a temporary cessation of hostilities

Vietnam War – (1955–1975) a civil war between North and South Vietnam, in which other powers, notably the USA and China, were involved

Answers

Pages 4–7: 'A Poison Tree'

QUICK TEST

1. He talks to the friend about his anger but does not tell his enemy.
2. It shows the softness of his behaviour in contrast with his deceit.
3. They were expelled from the Garden of Eden.
4. It has poisoned his soul, making him more angry and causing him to kill.

EXAM PRACTICE

Ideas might include the antithesis of his actions towards his enemy and his friend, the use of images of cultivation and the extended metaphor of the tree, how his anger has made him 'deceitful', and the shock of the final image and the speaker's reaction to his foe's death.

Pages 8–11: 'The Destruction of Sennacherib'

QUICK TEST

1. He is compared to a wolf because he is a ruthless predator.
2. From being strong and hopeful as they attack, they lie dead, scattered on the ground.
3. Banners, lances and a trumpet.
4. 'Melted like snow'.

EXAM PRACTICE

Ideas might include the simile of the leaves conveying the finality of their defeat, the 'Angel of Death' as God's avenging power, the ease with which the Assyrians are defeated, the contrast of their former 'might' with their destruction, and the use of the final simile to celebrate the power of 'the Lord'.

Pages 12–16: Extract from 'The Prelude'

QUICK TEST

1. He feels excited but guilty.
2. A swan and an elf.
3. He uses personification and repetition. He uses a caesura to mark the change in the way he rows.
4. He no longer sees nature as gentle, but as powerful and frightening.

EXAM PRACTICE

Ideas might include the literal imagery of its beauty and vastness, his feeling of being in control when the boat is like a 'swan', the personification of the 'huge peak', the feeling that it comes between him and the stars, the sense that it is pursuing him, and his reflection on the awe and fear he feels about its 'huge and mighty forms'.

Pages 17–20: 'The Man He Killed'

QUICK TEST

1. He uses speech marks and colloquial language.
2. 'Infantry'.
3. He was his foe (enemy).
4. He was unemployed and lived in the country, possibly a gamekeeper or a poacher.

EXAM PRACTICE

Ideas might include how 'face to face' gives the impression of close combat, the sense of 'kill or be killed', the lack of emotion, the acceptance that someone is an enemy, and the use of colloquial language to express both the ordinariness and the pointlessness of war.

Pages 21–25: 'Cousin Kate'

QUICK TEST

1. 'Wore', 'knot' and 'glove'.
2. It is pure, free and a symbol of peace.
3. Her cousin Kate, and her son.
4. He is more valuable than anything the lord has given Kate.

EXAM PRACTICE

Ideas might include the rhetorical questioning implying that his attention was flattering but led to sadness, the oxymoron of 'shameless shameful', the implication that he sees her as an object yet values her, and her pride in her love for him as well as in her son, the result of that love.

Pages 26–30: 'Half-caste'

QUICK TEST

1. 'Explain yuself'.
2. They show that mixing different colours can produce something complete and beautiful.
3. They imply that English people are as miserable and 'spiteful' as their weather.
4. That they are not open-minded and need things explained to them.

EXAM PRACTICE

Ideas might include how he repeatedly challenges the listener/reader to defend the use of the term, his use of positive images from art and music, and humour derived from the idea of being 'half' a person.

Pages 31–35: 'Exposure'

QUICK TEST

1. 'Knive' and 'tugging'.
2. 'But nothing happens'.
3. It is usually symbolic of hope but here brings suffering and death.
4. The image of the doors and shutters closed against them.

EXAM PRACTICE

Ideas might include the personification of the wind as a violent enemy, the refrain showing how things do not change, the association of war with bad weather, the fact that it is the weather that will kill them, the personification of the snow, the connotation of suffering animals as they 'cringe in holes', the repetition of 'dying' and the foretelling of their death from exposure in the last stanza.

Pages 36–40: 'The Charge of the Light Brigade'

QUICK TEST

1. He uses a strong regular (mainly dactylic) metre and repetition.
2. They are not 'dismay'd' and do not question the orders.
3. He uses a series of active verbs.
4. 'Honour'

EXAM PRACTICE

Ideas might include the use of repetition and anaphora, the strong regular rhythm, the constant threat of death, the personification of hell and death, the statement that 'Some one had blunder'd' suggesting the tragedy is unnecessary, the use of alliteration, and the imperatives at the end telling the reader how to react.

Pages 41–44: 'Catrin'

QUICK TEST

1. Any three from 'fierce', 'confrontation', 'fought', 'fighting', 'struggle' and 'defiant'.
2. Graffiti and/or poetry.
3. The umbilical cord.
4. It suggests that she feels that they are bound together forever by love and nature.

EXAM PRACTICE

Ideas might include the poet addressing her daughter as 'child', the imagery of conflict used to describe childbirth, the dominant image of the rope and its connotations, the feeling that the struggle continues, and her ambivalent attitude to their bond.

Pages 45–48: 'War Photographer'

QUICK TEST

1. People might think that because it is an isolated image, it is unusual or they might see it as something real if it is positive and 'lifts the heart'.
2. 'Sun-gilded', 'silk', 'champagne'.
3. A caesura marked by a semi-colon marks the start of the action and a full-stop, end-stopping the stanza, marks its conclusion.
4. The events after the taking of the photograph do not support the idea that the human spirit has triumphed.

EXAM PRACTICE

Ideas might include the different ways in which a photograph can reassure, the contrast between the photograph of Ascot and the war photograph, the ambiguity of the images of Ascot, the way in which a photograph captures a moment without reference to context, the difference between the photographer's experience and the headline and the final images of the blood showing how 'untidy' life is.

Pages 49–52: 'Belfast Confetti'

QUICK TEST

1. It is used to express strong feelings, such as shock or surprise.
2. Asterisk, hyphen, full stop, colon and question mark.
3. It is a maze that is difficult to escape from. In classical mythology it housed a deadly monster (the Minotaur).
4. They refer to the poet's sense of identity, questioning his past and his future.

EXAM PRACTICE

Ideas might include the use of punctuation as metaphors, the actual use of punctuation, use of caesura to break up lines, connotations of the street names, the impact of the names of the soldiers' equipment and the impact of the final rhetorical questions.

Pages 53–56: 'The Class Game'

QUICK TEST

1. It is a childish idea and/or it is a source of conflict.
2. Any three from "Olly', 'me' (for 'my'), 'Tara', "cos', 'corpy', 'bum' and 'bog'.
3. S/he is middle-class, lives in a semi-detached house on the Wirral and commutes to work in Liverpool.
4. You might think she is proud, defiant or even aggressive.

EXAM PRACTICE

Ideas might include the use of questions, use of dialect expressions contrasted with Standard English, antithesis, assonance in 'Does it stick in your gullet like a sour plum?', stereotypical examples of working-class life and the declaration of pride at the end.

Pages 57–61: 'Poppies'

QUICK TEST

1. It is set in a churchyard close to Armistice Sunday, reminding the speaker of those who have died in wars.
2. War and sewing.
3. It could represent her son's freedom or the release of her emotions.
4. Her son.

EXAM PRACTICE

Ideas might include the significance of memories of the son's childhood, the affectionate tone, the connotations of freeing the bird, use of metaphors connected with sewing, the impact of the first-person voice and the ambiguity of the final lines.

Pages 62–65: 'No Problem'

QUICK TEST

1. He uses dialect and refers to being the victim of racism.
2. They are athletic, can dance, and smile.
3. It shows that the speaker is knowledgeable and refers to a black civilisation.
4. The speaker reflects thoughtfully on his experience.

EXAM PRACTICE

Ideas might include the use of the first person, repetition of 'I am not de problem', use of dialect, rhyme and rhythm, use of patronising stereotypes, direct address to Britain and the connotations of 'Mother Country', and the poem's humorous tone.

Pages 66–69: 'What Were They Like?'

QUICK TEST

1. It is like a questionnaire, perhaps related to a report or thesis.
2. Children are like buds but the Vietnamese children have been killed in the war so cannot blossom.
3. 'Burned' and 'charred'.
4. The water on the paddy fields and the people's ability to reflect on their lives.

EXAM PRACTICE

Ideas might include the use of question and answer, the use of formal language, the stone of the lanterns used as metaphor, the association of children with blossoms, the harshness of the passive verbs, the double meaning of the mirror metaphor and the eerie calm created by 'silent' in the final line.

Pages 70–75: How To Compare Poetry

QUICK TEST

1. Two
2. Think about which poems have a similar theme. Choose one that you know well, has several similarities and/or differences, and that you can write enthusiastically about.
3. Compare them throughout the essay.
4. Establish a point of comparison.

EXAM PRACTICE

You could focus on the speakers, the difference in the emotions, the reasons/lack of reasons for the emotions, the idea of the 'foe', the use of imagery, the biblical/fairy-tale elements or the poets' use of ballad form.

Use the flow chart on page 73 to check that your writing follows the comparison structure described there.

Pages 81–83: Planning a Poetry Response

QUICK TEST

1. Language, form, structure and context.
2. It focuses your thoughts and helps you to write a well-structured essay.
3. Choose an appropriate poem.

EXAM PRACTICE

Choices for comparison might include 'The Destruction of Sennacherib', 'The Prelude', 'The Charge of the Light Brigade', 'Exposure' and 'What Were They Like?'. You could also argue that 'The Class Game', 'No Problem', 'Catrin' and 'Poppies' are about vulnerability. Ideas for comparison might include what is meant by vulnerability and what kind of vulnerability is presented, the situations that create vulnerability, and the reactions and attitudes of the poets/speakers to being vulnerable. You should have included brief references to how these elements are conveyed by the poets' choices of language, structure and form, and the relevance of contexts.

Pages 84–88: Grade 5 and Grade 7+ Annotated Responses

EXAM PRACTICE

Use the mark scheme below to assess your strengths and weaknesses. Work up from the bottom, putting a tick by the things you have fully accomplished and '½' by skills that are present but need development. Underline areas that need particular attention. Estimated grade boundaries are included to help you assess progress towards your target grade.

Approximate grade	Comparison	AO2 (15 marks)	AO3 (5 marks)
6–7+	Compares and contrasts the poems effectively, considering a wide and varied range of similarities and/or differences.	Sustained analysis of form and structure and their effect. Effective evaluation of the poets' use of language and its effect. Accurate and relevant subject terminology used to develop ideas.	Sustained comment on relevant context and understanding of the relationship between poems and context, integrated into the response.
4–5	Compares and contrasts a range of points, considering differences and/or similarities.	Shows a sound understanding of form and structure, linking them to their effect. Clear awareness, with relevant examples, of the poets' use of language and its effect. Relevant subject terminology used.	Sound comment on relevant context and its relationship to the poems.
2–3	Some comparisons and contrasts made.	Some comment on the form and structure of the poems. Some awareness of the poets' use of language, but without development. Limited use of relevant subject terminology.	Some awareness of context and some comment on its relationship to the poems.

This table can also be used to help you assess any other practice questions you have attempted.